THE
CUSTOMER
SIGNS YOUR
PAYCHECK

THE CUSTOMER SIGNS YOUR PAYCHECK

FRANK COOPER

McGraw-Hill

New York   Chicago   San Francisco
Lisbon   London   Madrid   Mexico City
Milan   New Delhi   San Juan   Seoul
Singapore   Sydney   Toronto

The **McGraw·Hill** Companies

1 2 3 4 5 6 7 8 9 0   DOC/DOC   0 1 0 9

ISBN   978-0-07-163288-1
MHID   0-07-163288-3

McGraw-Hill books are available at special quantity discounts to use as premiums and sales promotions, or for use in corporate training programs. To contact a representative, please e-mail us at bulksales@mcgraw-hill.com.

This book is printed on acid-free paper.

Library of Congress Cataloging-in-Publication Data
Cooper, Frank (Frank J.), 1938–
    The customer signs your paycheck / by Frank Cooper.
        p. cm.
    ISBN 0-07-163288-3 (alk. paper)
1. Customer relations.   2. Customer services.   3. Consumer satisfaction.   I. Title.
    HF5415.5.C664 2010
    658.8'12—dc22   2009011277

This book is dedicated to the girl I married in 1957,
the mother of our six children, the world's best grandma,
my business partner, my traveling companion, my adviser . . .
and the best friend I ever had—Arnene A. Cooper.

CONTENTS

THE CUSTOMER SIGNS YOUR PAYCHECK

Part 1

You and Your Company

Chapter 1

POISE AND CONFIDENCE IN CUSTOMER RELATIONS

Have you ever wondered why the people at your company hired YOU? They probably could have chosen someone else if they had wanted to . . . but they didn't! They saw personal traits in you that are important to the company's image, and then hired you to help present that image to the public.

When you were interviewed for your job, the person who made the decision to hire you was looking for specific personal qualities from among job applicants. Every business knows that its success in the marketplace can be greatly enhanced by hiring the "right" people. The *hiring decision* is one of the most expensive decisions that a company makes if you consider the cost of training a new employee and the total amount of wages and benefits that will be paid during the entire time of employment. But even more important is the question, "How will this new employee affect our customer relations?"

KEY CONCEPT #1

You as an employee are one of your company's most valuable assets.

When it comes to customer relations, your greatest strength will always be in the uniqueness of your personality. When you let your personality shine forth, you do a tremendous favor for your company. It makes people—customers—feel good about doing business with you. There really is magic in your personality! You have a personality that cannot, and will not, ever be duplicated. And your unique personality carries with it your own special pattern for success in whatever you do in life.

The only thing necessary to let the power of your personality shine forth is to *accept* yourself and to *like* yourself. People who like themselves seem to have an easier time with whatever they do. They are the people who take a good look at themselves and decide that the only people they can ever be *are themselves*, and they learn to accept and appreciate who they are. They build on their strengths rather than compensate for their weaknesses. They become themselves rather than trying to become someone else. And it feels good!

Now you'd think that this business of *liking yourself* might be pretty easy. Well, it is for some people. People who were fortunate enough to have parents who kept telling them they were OK learned to believe in themselves early in life. But it seems that most of us pick up mistaken notions about ourselves during our formative years as our attention is drawn to the need for improvement. We grow up learning to identify our shortcomings much more easily than our good qualities.

Another stumbling block to self-appreciation is the mistaken idea that we must be *perfect* at all times. Nobody's perfect. Each of us is OK, but not perfect. Life would be pretty dull if we all were perfect, wouldn't it? We must settle for being OK, realizing that we do make mistakes as we learn. Being imperfect is a sign of vitality, because it is a sign of growth potential, and growth is the only sign of life! If we are green, we are growing; if we are ripe, we are rotting. Perfect is ripe.

When you make a mistake, it is important that you take responsibility for the error immediately rather than find excuses or try to "fix the blame" on someone or something else. The sooner you admit to a mistake, the sooner you profit by it, and the sooner you're happy again. Admit the mistake, correct it if you can, and get on with life.

Everyone has occasional experiences on the job that have negative effects on poise and self-confidence. It could be a corrective reprimand from a supervisor, a difficult customer, or some other uncomfortable situation that leaves the person feeling "down." The temptation at these times might be to complain bitterly to fellow employees or to other customers, but this would be a mistake that could have significant negative results. When we complain, we sow the seeds of negativity in our work environment, and when those negative seeds sprout and grow, we find ourselves not enjoying life very much. We're much better off if we handle difficult situations in a positive manner and then try to learn what kind of action can improve our future performance.

Remember, if you are conscientiously trying to do your best work and be the best person you can be, there is absolutely no reason why you should ever feel "second rate." The world's population is now in the billions, but among those billions there is not one person who is more important than you are. We're all in this together! When your poise and self-confidence get shaken, pick yourself up, brush yourself off, and move on. Handle reprimands and difficult customers as opportunities to learn more about people and life in general, and as a result you will discover that life gets easier.

And finally, don't you just love to be around people who like themselves? They're the kind of people who know that they are OK and don't have to go through life trying to prove it to themselves and to others. Liking yourself is often a question of "Why not?" Who else can you be? You've got what it takes, and you don't have to add one thing to yourself. *You just have to let it happen.*

"When it comes to customer relations, your greatest strength will always be in the uniqueness of your personality."

Chapter 2

YOU ARE A CUSTOMER, TOO

The best way to understand good customer relations is to pause for a moment and consider your own experience as a customer. You are a customer almost every day of your life. How do you like to be treated when you are making a purchase? What kind of attitude do you appreciate in a clerk or salesperson when it is *your money* that will be pushed across the counter in exchange for a product or service?

Can you recall a recent incident in which you were treated incorrectly as a customer? Is there a particular place where you avoid doing business because of the way you are treated as a customer?

As you read this book, you will begin to develop a new perspective on every business transaction. In fact you will see living proof of this book's pages in your almost daily experience as a customer. Examine these experiences, and you will continue to develop a strong sense of what it takes to be successful in customer relations in the *real* world of business.

KEY CONCEPT #2

Use your own experience as a customer to help you understand the principles of good customer relations.

As an employee, you have an excellent opportunity to enhance the quality of your own life by learning and applying the concepts of good customer relations. Considering the number of hours you spend on the job, you realize that a significant portion of your lifetime takes place at work! If your time with customers is pleasant, then your life is more enjoyable. Don't you agree?

There's a law that governs your success, no matter where you go or what you do. It's called the *law of cause and effect*. This law states that for every *action* there will always be a predictable *reaction*. The law of cause and effect applies to customer relations, too. When you make customers happy, you become happier yourself.

Three Legs of Customer Relations

There are three legs to good customer relations, and just like a three-legged stool, if one of the legs is missing, the stool will topple. The successful employee is the person who gives diligent attention to each of these three components.

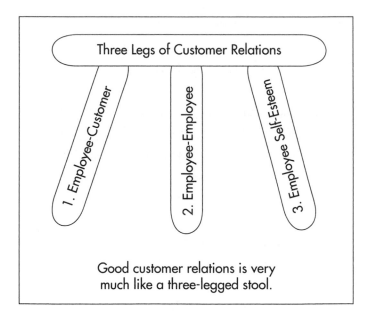

Three Legs of Customer Relations

1. Employee-Customer

2. Employee-Employee

3. Employee Self-Esteem

Good customer relations is very much like a three-legged stool.

> **KEY CONCEPT #3**
>
> The three legs of customer relations are:
> 1. The relationship that exists between the employee and the customer
> 2. The relationship that exists between the employee and fellow employees
> 3. The self-esteem of the employee

1. **Customer relations is *human relations*.** It is a bond or connection between two or more people during which they exchange attention and communicate messages. Not all of the messages are communicated with *words*. Much of the communication is nonverbal and extra-verbal. The quality of this communication determines the quality of the relationship between the employee and the customer.

2. **The relationship that exists among employees in a business is extremely important to the customer's impression of the business.** Customers have an intuitive ability to pick up on how well people are getting along with one another at your place of business. It's not the sort of thing that customers ponder and then reach logical conclusions about, but rather it's something they have *feelings* about.

Perhaps you've had the experience of visiting a store or restaurant where employees were not getting along with one another. What was the feeling that you had about being there? You probably would have enjoyed yourself more if the employees were happier.

3. **Every person has a self-image, or mental picture, of who he or she is.** The mental picture begins to develop early in the person's life and continues to change as the person discovers more about himself or herself. It's this self-image that dictates a person's behavior. It's as though a person's self-image becomes a *script* for the person to follow in any given situation.

A successful person has a wholesome self-image and *simply acts out that self-image on life's stage.* It's a well-known fact that we become who we think we are, so to improve our performances we must begin by developing mental pictures of ourselves as high performers. This book will help you develop your own mental picture of a person who is successful at customer relations.

Employees who accept themselves are said to have a positive self-image. I'm not speaking of vanity, self-centeredness, or feelings of superiority. I'm speaking of the person who recognizes his or her own self-worth, feels comfortable with who he or she is, and has reached a sense of self-acceptance. If you call to mind a particular person that you always enjoy visiting, chances are that same person has the kind of self-image we're discussing here. It is the same positive self-image that makes for good customer relations.

A large number of businesses are failing every day. The number is staggering. The list of reasons for failure in business could probably fill several pages, but most of them would boil down to just one reason: *not enough customers!* Without enough customers, the lifeblood of any business is cut off.

The smartest businesses soon learn the importance of repeat business, which means that these companies take steps to make certain that their customers are happy enough to return for additional purchases and to recommend the business to friends. For a business to succeed, its employees must realize that there is no such thing as a single sale. Every time a customer is satisfied, the likelihood for additional purchases is assured.

KEY CONCEPT #4

In the long run, repeat business depends upon customer satisfaction.

Here are some of the reasons why so much attention must be given to customer satisfaction:

1. The customer is the real reason that your company is in business in the first place. Every product and service is designed with the customer in mind.

2. It is the customer who will determine whether your business will prosper and grow. Your business may have dreams and plans for the future, but it will be the customer who determines whether those dreams come true.

3. The customer tells a business which products and services it can sell. People seldom buy things for which they have no need. The successful business must be keenly aware of customers' needs.

4. The customer pays every employee's wages, plus the rent, plus the utilities, and every other bill the business receives. Money is the lifeblood of every business, and every dollar it receives comes from the customer's pocket.

5. A satisfied customer is the most effective and least expensive form of business advertising. How many times have you purchased a product or service from a particular company because someone gave you an enthusiastic recommendation?

"When you make customers happy, you become happier yourself."

Chapter 3

ATTITUDES THAT HELP YOU GET AHEAD

As you consider your personal success with customers, you need to realize that your attitude is more important than your knowledge or experience. Although it's necessary to add to your knowledge every day, it's your attitude that will carry you to the top in any organization.

Here are some attitudes that will help you get ahead wherever you go.

1. Think Like the Boss

When you try to look at things through the eyes of your manager or supervisor, you accomplish two very important goals. You develop the kind of outlook that grooms you for advancement, and you become more valuable to your company. When you begin to think like the boss, it shows in your behavior, and it increases the amount of enjoyment you derive from your job.

Imagine, if you will, how your manager or supervisor looks at things. If you do this, it will be easy to understand how the boss sees things just a little differently from other employees.

Every decision you make as an employee will give you an opportunity to look at the situation through the eyes of the boss. If you ask yourself, "What would my decision be if I were owner of the company?" then you've taken your first step toward thinking like the boss.

For example, let's say a customer has a question about an item that is for sale. The employee who thinks like the boss is more tuned in to answering the customer's question in a way that shows the business is interested in earning the customer's satisfaction, goodwill, and loyalty. The employee who *doesn't* think like the boss is more apt to demonstrate a little more indifference toward the customer.

2. Be a Problem Finder

Anyone can be a *problem solver*, but the most valuable employees are the ones who are *problem finders*. Problem finders have their antennae up and are acutely aware of what's going on in their surroundings.

A surprising number of employees will notice but ignore things that go wrong. They'll walk right past something that needs to be fixed. They mean no harm; they just aren't thinking in terms of correcting things that need to be corrected.

Many business problems result in waste, inefficiency, and additional expense. Problem finders are important to a business because they save time and money, and they usually help the business find better methods for getting things done.

Let's say, for example, that an employee notices the company is running out of business stationery. The company's stationery isn't printed very often, so it's the sort of thing that doesn't get much attention. The problem finder, upon noticing that the stationery supply is getting low, mentions it to the person responsible for reordering it. The non-problem finder might also see that the supply is getting low but doesn't think to mention it to anyone. The non-problem finder thinks, "Stationery is not my job."

In your opinion, which employee is more valuable to the business?

3. Be 100 Percent Loyal

I encourage you to develop a loyal attitude toward your company and the people who run it. By doing so, you will become one of your company's most valuable assets.

No person can be *for* something and *against* it at the same time. The loyal employee is *for* the company, and the disloyal employee is *against* it.

I am dismayed by the number of employees who make negative comments about their employers. No employer is perfect. So what?

People who make negative comments about their places of employment hurt themselves in the long run because their attitudes diminish the quality of their lives, and they hurt their reputations in the eyes of those who hear their negative comments.

When customers hear disloyal comments from a company's employees, they begin to lose confidence in the company and are less apt to do business with it. As a result, the company suffers . . . and when a company suffers, its employees suffer.

4. Be Enthusiastic!

I would be willing to bet that the 10 most successful people you know are also the 10 most enthusiastic.

Employees who are enthusiastic about job-related matters have an easier time getting things done, energize the workplace, earn the support and cooperation of fellow workers, and are less stressed at the end of the workday. Winners are enthusiastic!

Enthusiasm is a *choice*. For an experiment, the next time you arrive at your place of business, give your fellow workers a positive and enthusiastic greeting and put a little spring in your step. Chances are, your job will be more fun that day.

5. Do More Than You Get Paid For

Every job carries with it expectations for fulfillment. Many employees just do their jobs and let it go at that. Their attitude is, "I do what I get paid for. That's why the company hired me." These employees are fine folks, but they're only *average*.

Successful people are the ones who do just a little more than others expect. They stand out as "extra milers," and as a result, they rise to the top within any organization.

Ask yourself, "What are a few ways I can do a little more than is expected of me?" You'll be surprised at how easily the answer comes to you. You'll notice your extra-mile ideas don't require much more effort and energy. If you find ways to do just a little bit extra on the job, you will notice that your work is both more rewarding and more creative.

6. Fix the Problem, Not the Blame

When things go wrong (and they will), focus your energy on fixing the problem rather than on fixing the blame. People who spend their time blaming one another for mistakes just waste their time, and they diminish the quality of their work lives. You deserve better.

In companies where there's a lot of finger-pointing, employees tend to worry too much about making mistakes, and people who worry about making mistakes usually make more of them.

In a blame-ridden workplace people often *hide* their mistakes. For obvious reasons this creates additional problems, and it results in shoddy products and services. When this happens, customers, employers, and employees become the real losers.

7. Don't Talk About People

Have you ever been associated with a group of people whose major topic of conversation was other people? If so, you probably got the impression that you were the topic of conversation when you were away.

If this was the case, you then became cautious about what you said or did while with the group. If it was a work group, you then took fewer risks, and as a result you became less creative and innovative.

Today, more than ever before, companies need employees who are willing to take risks, use their imaginations, and come up with new ways of doing things. And this only happens in work environments in which employees are confident they are not being talked about behind their backs.

In addition, customers who visit a place of business don't like to hear employees talking about one another or about things that are going on among one another. It makes them feel uncomfortable, and if the comments are the least bit negative, it drives them away.

8. Be 100 Percent Honest

During the course of any workday, most employees have the opportunity to be less than 100 percent honest because they have access to the company's money, property, and merchandise.

I encourage you to maintain a high level of honesty at work. Do the "right thing because it's the right thing." I guarantee it'll pay off in big dividends for you sooner or later.

Occasionally an employee will think: "The company will never miss it. It's no big deal. I'll just go ahead and take it." Unwittingly the employee thereby steps over the line and becomes a thief.

People who live by one set of values among friends and family and by a compromised set of values at their places of employment are only fooling themselves. Stealing in one place is the same as stealing in another. It doesn't make sense to think otherwise.

KEY CONCEPT #5

Attitudes that help you get ahead:
1. **Think like the boss.**
2. **Be a problem finder.**

---

3. Be 100 percent loyal.

4. Be enthusiastic!

5. Do more than you get paid for.

6. Fix the problem, not the blame.

7. Don't talk about people.

8. Be 100 percent honest.

Part 2

Ten Commandments for Customer Relations

Ten Commandments for Customer Relations

1. **The customer is never an interruption.**

   The customer is your real reason for being in business. Chores can wait!

2. **Greet every customer with a friendly smile.**

   Customers are people, and they like friendly contact. They usually return it.

3. **Call customers by name.**

   Make a game of learning customers' names. See how many you can remember. This is a valuable habit.

4. **Remember, you are the company.**

   In the customer's eyes, you are as important as the president of your company . . . probably even more so.

5. **Never argue with a customer.**

   Customers are always right (in their own eyes). Be a good listener, agree with your customers where you can, and then do what you can to make them happy.

6. **Never say "I don't know."**

   If you don't know the answer to a customer's question, say, "That's a good question. Let me see if I can find out for you."

7. The customer pays your wages.

Every dollar you earn comes from the customer's pocket. Treat the customer like the boss. It's the customer who signs your paycheck.

8. State things in a positive way.

Choose positive words when speaking to customers. It takes practice, but it is a valuable habit that will help you become an effective communicator.

9. Brighten every customer's day.

Make it a point to do something that brings a little sunshine into each customer's life, and soon you'll discover that your own life is happier and brighter!

10. Always go the extra mile.

Always do just a little more than the customer expects you to do. You will be richly rewarded for this habit.

Chapter 4

THE CUSTOMER IS NEVER AN INTERRUPTION

Most retail and service-related jobs include some responsibility for additional tasks, such as keeping your work area clean, straightening merchandise, and doing backup work. These are chores that must be done by someone, and they are generally part of the job description of the person who must also tend to the needs of customers. A retail or service business would not be considered successful if these extra chores were neglected.

Getting these additional tasks completed can become a problem in more ways than one. The employee who is responsible for doing the chores is likely to be scheduled for a specific number of hours during the shift, and within this time frame, he or she is expected to complete all side work. During times when business is especially good and the company is serving a large number of customers, the frustration of having to do the additional work can create an uncomfortable situation for the employee who wants to do a good job.

As a customer, yourself, you may have had the experience of visiting a place of business where you intended to make a purchase. As you entered the establishment, you may have noticed that the sales clerk was busily restocking merchandise or sweeping the floor . . . and at the moment you caught his glance, a look of disappointment and exasperation came over his face as he "greeted" you. How did you feel as a customer during this experience? Chances are, you felt bothered and as though you came at the wrong time.

Customers don't like to feel as though they are intruding by showing up at the wrong time. Although it might not be a strong feeling of embarrassment, they will still have a slight feeling of discomfort—similar to what you feel when you realize that you've phoned a friend right in the middle of his or her family dinner.

When customers are treated as though they are an interruption to your work, they feel as though they are not very important. In other words, when customers get the message that they are an intrusion on chores, they tend to think the chores are more important than they are. And you can't blame them for feeling this way if the employee looked sorry to see them.

Customers—because they are people—need to feel important. Customers must never get the impression that they are less important than other factors in your business. If customers feel embarrassed because they think they visited your business at the wrong time, they are likely to stay away from your business in the future. People do not like to go where they are not welcome.

Also, it is a good idea to remember that when your doors are open, *you are open for business*! Too often, customers will visit a business establishment 10 or 15 minutes before closing time, and they get the impression they came at the wrong time because all the employees are involved in the work of closing up for the day. The message the customers get is that they came to the establishment *after normal business hours* and that they better not be serious about buying anything because it might create a problem.

KEY CONCEPT #6

There is never a "wrong" time to serve a customer if your doors are open for business.

Every business is created with one thought in mind: "Provide a needed product or service to customers." The customer *is the reason* you're in business. Every chore, every task, every other activity must come second to serving the customer. Whenever the customer is put second, the business suffers.

Treat all customers as though you are really happy to see them, almost as though you had actually hoped they would come in today. Give them the impression that your reason for being there is to serve them, and you will help your business grow and prosper.

Chapter 5

GREET EVERY CUSTOMER WITH A FRIENDLY SMILE

Most of us understand the power of a smile, but too often we forget. The smile is one of our world's most underused sources of power. It can bring radiance and energy to virtually every situation. When we greet customers with a friendly smile, we nearly guarantee that serving them will be a positive experience!

Smiles are contagious! They spread faster than the common cold. As the song says, "When you're smiling, the whole world smiles with you!" If you would like to try an easy and interesting experiment, do this: smile at the next five people you happen to meet—friends, family, anyone—and see what happens. Go ahead and do it. It'll be fun, and you'll witness firsthand the positive power that you can have on people by simply taking the time to smile.

Some people don't know how to smile. They think it's done with the teeth! They couldn't be more mistaken. Perhaps you have seen someone with a smile on his mouth and a bored expression in his eyes. Smiling is done *with the eyes*! And it is easy to do . . . it requires two-thirds fewer muscles than frowning does. You actually save energy when you smile instead of frown.

KEY CONCEPT #7

When smiling at a customer, put the look of "I like you!" in your eyes. The rest of your face will then fall into place naturally.

Let's say that the typical customer walks into your place of business. The likelihood is that she has the ordinary "ups and downs" that we all have and that life for her that day has been a mixture of pluses and minuses. Since most people consider themselves to be busy, she is probably preoccupied with the day's activities, and maybe even a little impatient. In order to get off on the right foot with this customer, it will be absolutely necessary for you to establish friendly contact with her as soon as you can, even if you are busy with another customer. Always make eye contact with customers as soon as possible, and with a smile in your eyes that says "Hello." It only takes a second.

Customers have needs that go beyond your products and services. *They need to know that you know they exist!* No one likes to be ignored, and one of the finest ways to make customers feel important is to acknowledge their presence as soon as you can. This friendly acknowledgment will provide customers with the patience they need if there is going to be a short delay in service.

Employees, especially new ones, become overly concerned about how to greet customers in a way that lets the customers know the employees are there to provide assistance. Some employers tell their employees to say, "Can I help you?" and other employers say, "For goodness sakes—whatever you do—*don't* walk up to a customer and say, 'Can I help you?' Customers want help, or they wouldn't be here!" The best way to make customers feel at home is to greet them as though they were friends. After all, customers are the most important friends your business has. If customers are greeted in this manner, they'll probably let you know why they're there.

If a customer comes into a retail outlet and says "I'm just looking," let the person look. Lookers become buyers if they aren't pushed too hard. Individual customers have different styles of shopping. Some customers want lots of help and attention, while others do not. The important thing to remember is that every customer must feel comfortable at your place of business. You must be alert to "reading" customers to determine what kind of shoppers they are, *and then you need to adapt to their pattern*. Don't try to make customers fit into your pattern . . . it might not fit their style, and they'll become uncomfortable.

KEY CONCEPT #8

People must feel comfortable when doing business with you. Adapt to their style as best you can. Be alert and flexible in your approach to customers.

When customers bring friends or family members to your place of business, it is important that each member of the party be acknowledged by a greeting, or at least with eye contact. Be especially nice to the children of customers. Giving them extra attention can pay big dividends. Not only will you be winning future customers for your business, but when children receive a lot of positive attention, they seldom need to seek negative attention by acting up. When children misbehave in a place of business, it generally makes their parents feel uncomfortable—and eager to leave. Do what you can to make *everyone in the family* feel good about being there.

When the time comes for your customers to leave your place of business, always remember to say good-bye as though you were speaking to a friendly acquaintance whom you intend to see again. This farewell does not have to be a dramatic event, but it should make customers feel as though they are always welcome. This last impression customers receive will influence them in the future. People are motivated to return to places where they feel comfortable and where they have a sense of belonging.

"When we greet customers
with a friendly smile, we nearly
guarantee that serving them will
be a positive experience!"

Chapter 6

CALL CUSTOMERS BY NAME

Have you ever had someone call you by name when you least expected it? Perhaps it was a time when you were walking down the street, or standing in an elevator, or walking into a place of business, and someone caught your glance and greeted you by using your name. How did it make you feel? Were you curious, interested, puzzled, pleased, . . .? Well, one thing's for certain—the person who called you by name had your attention!

In today's crowded and sometimes hectic business environment, more and more people show indifference toward one another. This can be easily demonstrated by walking down a busy street and observing passersby. Notice how many of them carry blank expressions on their faces, staring straight ahead, reluctant to look at other people. This is really a type of loneliness.

People really do have a need to *belong*. Each of us is motivated by a desire to be accepted and to eliminate loneliness from our lives. It feels good for us to be in a familiar place where people know us and call us by name. Some marvelous things happen to us when we experience acceptance. We feel comfortable; we want to linger; we want to return to the places that create good feelings in us.

You can make customers feel good about visiting your place of business when you call them by name as you greet them. You're probably thinking, "That's fine, but it's difficult for me to remember names." Actually, remembering names is easy, once you know how. It's a simple matter of learning some rules for success.

Here are four easy-to-learn rules that will help you develop the skill of remembering names. You notice I call this a *skill*, not a *talent*. Imagine the fun you will have once you put this new skill to work for you. And the best thing about it is that you can begin today!

KEY CONCEPT #9

The four rules for remembering names are:
1. **You must *desire* to remember names.**
2. **You must *learn* the names you want to remember.**

> 3. You must *repeat* the names you want to remember.
> 4. You must *associate* the names with something.

How to Remember Names

1. Desire

Desire is a powerful motivator. It helps you take careful aim at what you want and then impels you to action.

When you desire to remember names, you begin to focus your attention on the *activity* of remembering names. Without the desire, it will never happen. Right now, you need to analyze your desire to remember names. Is the desire strong enough to get you moving? If it's not, then picture yourself as the person who has developed this valuable skill. Imagine the first few times that you actually remember a customer's name and greet that customer with a friendly smile and call him or her by name. Imagine the look of pleased surprise on the customer's face as he or she returns your attention. It'll be fun!

2. Learn

The most obvious rule is that you must *learn* a name if you are ever going to remember it. This may sound simple, but how many times have you been introduced to someone, and the person's name flew right past you because you were not paying close enough attention. You might have been preoccupied with what you were going to say or had given in to some other distracting thought. It's perfectly normal to do this, and it happens quite often.

The *desire to remember names* will help you *learn* the names you want to remember. It will call for a conscious effort on your part. You must focus your attention on *getting the name* when you have the opportunity, either when introduced, or when it is placed on a sales order, or when the customer writes a check or pays with a credit card. These are all opportunities to learn a name.

If the name isn't presented to you in any of the ways mentioned above, then you must *go after the name*. In other words, use your own effort to find out the customer's name. This can sometimes be accomplished by casually introducing yourself to the customer. It is important to do this without being too aggressive. Another way to get a customer's name is by asking the customer in a polite manner or by asking someone else who may know the customer.

As you learn the customer's name, take a good look at the customer. Get a good, complete impression of the person's features, coloring, height, and anything else that is distinctive or different about the person. Pay attention to what the customer looks like so that it will be easy to recognize him or her in the future. Remember, the customer may be wearing different clothing next time, so focus your attention on personal features.

3. Repeat

Repeat the customer's name. In some respects you will be *memorizing* the name as you repeat it to yourself. As you are talking to the customer, repeat the name in your mind during pauses in the conversation or while the customer is looking at merchandise or is involved in another activity in your place of business.

Another way to repeat the name of the customer is to work it into the conversation with the customer. "This is one of our most popular items, Mrs. Brown." "Anything for dessert today, Mr. White?" "Thank you, Ms. Black."

Whether you call customers by their first names or more formally by their last names preceded by a Mr., Ms., or Mrs. should be determined by what's likely to make them feel at ease. Adult customers seldom appreciate aggressive familiarity from young people, so unless an adult customer indicates the first-name approach, stick with the more formal. Since everyone appreciates being respected, the safest approach with customers is to call them by their last names. It makes them feel more important, too.

Recite customers' names to yourself during the workday while you're doing chores such as straightening merchandise or tidying your work area. Make a game of seeing how many names you can learn and recite in one day. You will be repeating the names and doing one more thing that adds interest to your job.

4. Associate

Associate the customer's name with something that will help you remember the name in the future. By associating the name in this manner you visualize the object *along with the person* on your next encounter. Your logical mind then *connects* the two, and you remember the name.

Associating the name is the creative part of the recall process. And like all creative endeavors, there are no set rules or patterns to follow. You can conjure up some wild and offbeat objects, people, or places to associate with a person's name. Some of the associations will be complimentary to the individual, and some will not. And if a person should ever ask you what you associate his or her name with, I suggest that you refrain from mentioning unflattering name connections. I have learned this by experience . . . uncomfortable experience.

As you *learn* a customer's name, study the name for a meaning or any obvious connection to a thing. Some names can be associated with characteristics that the person has, such as height, weight, coloring, hair, shape of body, or posture. If the person's name is Mrs. Tower, associate the name with her height. If the person's name is Mr. Lightfoot, associate "Light" with weight or coloring, and of course "foot" with that part of the body. If the first name is Harry, associate it with the person's hair. In each case it's important to form a picture of the person whose name you want to remember along with the object you're using for association. In this way, the next time you see the person, you will also visualize the object of association. It works.

Some names can be readily associated with *places* or *things*. For instance, Mr. French can be associated with the country of France. Virginia can be associated with the state by the same name. Mrs. Fountaine can be linked with a fountain, and Frank can be connected to a hot dog.

Other names can be associated with occupations such as baker, cooper, smith, and potter. The opportunity to associate names is almost unlimited. You can also associate a person's name with another person who has the same name. Perhaps the new acquaintance's name is Kathy, and she reminds you of your sister Kathy. Once you make the link in your mind, it will come back to you in the future.

Some names can be associated with more than one object, such as the name Carson (*car* and *son*), Waterhouse (*water* and *house*), and Samuelson (*Sam* and *mule* and *son* or *sun*). These names lend themselves to the development of more complex mental pictures because they involve more than one item, but still the method works.

You will really have to get creative with some names such as Sattlemeier, Gerlach, and Westling, but with a little practice Sattlemeier (*saddle-in-my-ear*), Gerlach (bear making *Grrr* sound as he tries to open a *latch*), and Westling (*ling*cod swimming *west*ward) become easy to remember. Try it . . . it's fun!

Try your hand at associating the following names, using some of the guidelines mentioned earlier. Take your time and use your imagination. I think you will be surprised at how easy it is once you get started.

1. Brown
2. Bell
3. Kingshott

4. Tallman
5. Tackitt
6. Robin

7. Jack	14. Bill Harryman
8. Inkster	15. Ronald Moore
9. Nardinger	16. Amber Nichols
10. Rhodes	17. Mark Christianson
11. Holly Greenshield	18. Dexter Lampers
12. Candy Hart	19. Floyd Scanlan
13. Frank Cooper	20. Chester Krumstick

If you took the time to associate the names listed above, then you discovered that it becomes easier once you get started—and more fun—as your creativity is taxed by names that are not readily associated.

Remembering names is a skill that can be developed easily and quickly if the simple rules are followed: *desire* to remember names; *learn* the names you want to remember; *repeat* the names; and *associate* the names with places, things, occupations, characteristics, or other people. Begin today!

Chapter 7

REMEMBER, YOU ARE THE COMPANY

Retail and service businesses can be operated from virtually every type of building, ranging from the tall, richly appointed skyscraper to the lively shopping mall environment to the humble roadside stand. But without employees, a place of business would be nothing but a dull and lifeless building. A business is really *people* who are providing products, services, and sometimes ideas to other *people* who need them.

True, it's easier to succeed in a business that is properly located, is actively advertised, and has an appropriately designed setting. These and other important considerations help to ensure the prosperity of any business, but what gives *personality* to a business are the people who work there. The employees will be long remembered after a customer has forgotten the color of the paint on a store's walls.

It's important for all employees to take *genuine ownership* of their jobs and to develop the feeling of "we" rather than "they" when discussing their companies. Employees who identify strongly with their work are always happier at their jobs and become the most valuable resources their companies have. These effective people realize that they spend a significant part of their time (life!) on the job and want to make the most of it. I feel sorry for employees who *are just putting in time* on the job and are planning to start living at quitting time. These people are unhappy.

KEY CONCEPT #10

Develop a feeling of ownership for your job. It is your life while you are at work. Make the most of it. You will be happy and successful as a result.

There have been times when I visited retail and service outlets and was truly embarrassed for the owners of the businesses because of the attitudes of the employees. As I reflect on the source of my embarrassment, I realize it was because the employees didn't seem to care about the businesses at all, and their attitudes reflected indifference toward customers. It was sad.

On the other hand, I have visited businesses where the employees were enthusiastic about their companies. They didn't see their jobs as work . . . they were fun! They loved their jobs, and they found it easy to be successful in them. They were interested, lively, and animated. All this was possible because they decided to *become the businesses*! These were *their* jobs, *their* companies.

When customers visit your business, the most important impression they receive will be from the person who represents the business. They don't care who owns the company, nor do they care who your boss is. As far as they're concerned, *you are the company*. In their eyes, you are the most important person in the company because you are the person who is going to help them fill their needs.

Also, employees who are well groomed and appropriately attired give customers confidence in the business. Customers feel there is a "correctness" about the business. This is why dress codes and guidelines for personal appearance are important considerations for most companies.

Personal taste in clothing is important to every-one, including employees, but in some cases, and especially when an employee is representing the company, personal taste must yield to what's appropriate in the business setting. When employers enforce dress codes, they are correctly attempting to give their companies the images necessary for success—images that customers expect.

Chapter 8

NEVER ARGUE WITH A CUSTOMER

It is pointless to argue with a customer. The list of reasons why you should not is very long, and the list of reasons why you *should* doesn't exist! There is not one good thing to be gained by arguing with a customer, not even a "friendly argument," if you think there is such a thing.

When two people argue, they are really *fighting* with one another; it's just that they are using words instead of fists or weapons. This is why quarrels are destructive and always result in situations that have been worsened by the arguments.

The object of all businesses is to *serve* people, and the quality and volume of their service will determine how successful any enterprise will become. When customers get involved in arguments at places of business, it always results in less business for those establishments. If employees "win" arguments, they will most likely lose customers, and lost customers become an efficient form of negative advertising. People don't forget arguments, especially if they lose them. People who lose arguments lose face, and their egos are hurt. In order for them to get even, they must find ways to retaliate. Maybe it shouldn't be that way, but that's the way it is with human nature.

Some people (employees and customers alike) just love to argue. I don't know why, but it probably has something to do with their upbringing or self-image. These folks will argue about *anything*, and in some cases it doesn't matter to them which side they take. They just want to argue. They are not much fun to be with, and they seldom have many friends.

When you come in contact with a customer who seems to want to quarrel, remember that *it takes two people to argue*. When only one person argues, that person is not *in* an argument; *he or she is simply complaining!* An argument is like a drama that has two roles to it. The decision you must make is to refuse to play the role of the second party to the argument.

The best way to handle a customer who seems to be looking for a quarrel is to agree with the customer where you can, listen to whatever else the customer says, and ask questions about the person's point of view. The customer will feel as though he or she is "educating" you, even though you realize that this is not the case. This will make the customer feel important, because he or she probably has very few listeners. It is also the kindest thing to do, and it gives you one more reason to like yourself. After all, the thing that the customer wants to quarrel about seldom has any consequence on the quality of your life. And by listening, you might even be entertained . . . and most certainly you will learn a little more about human nature.

When a patron is voicing a *customer complaint*, it's much different from the quarrels discussed above. Customer complaints must be handled quickly and efficiently. If you have a dissatisfied customer on your hands, you want the length of time the customer is dissatisfied to be as short as possible. You also want to replace that dissatisfaction with *satisfaction*—and certainly *not* do anything that adds to the unhappiness!

KEY CONCEPT #11

Two things to remember when handling a customer complaint: handle the complaint quickly so the customer is dissatisfied for the shortest possible length of time, and don't do anything that will add to the customer's dissatisfaction.

I believe all problems have solutions, including the problems voiced in customer complaints, but it becomes frustrating if the solutions to those problems are outside of our control. Let's face it, there are some problems that *we* can't solve personally. In some cases, our responsibility to customers is not in *providing* solutions to complaints but rather in *finding* solutions.

If, for instance, the solution to a customer's complaint is outside the scope of your personal authority to resolve, then you must pass the problem up to the person who can solve the problem. This must be done as quickly as reasonably possible, and you must stay with the customer and the problem until you have reached the source of the solution. In doing this, you will be letting the customer know that the complaint has not been dropped along the way and that you will not be adding to the customer's frustration and dissatisfaction. Show the customer that you care.

When a customer complaint involves a request for a refund, or when the nature of the complaint will otherwise affect the income of your business, it is best to follow the policy of your employer concerning such matters. It is important that you *know* what your company's policies are in order to be able to handle these types of complaints quickly. If you have done what you can for the customer but he or she is still dissatisfied, then the best thing to do is to find a solution elsewhere. True, it can become difficult, but you want that customer's business in the future . . . and you also want to do business with the customer's family and friends!

Chapter 9

NEVER SAY
"I DON'T KNOW"

One of the most common and devastating mistakes employees make in replying to customer questions is found in the answer "I don't know." When a question is answered in this manner, it's generally interpreted by the customer to mean "I don't know, *and I don't care.*" It has a *final* sound about it, as though a dead end has been reached in the discussion.

The habit of replying to questions with "I don't know" is generally formed in childhood as a suitable reply to a parent's inquiry. When parents ask a child, "When are you going to get your work done?" or "What happened?" the answer that requires the least amount of effort is "I don't know." It also lightens the burden of responsibility, and it allows the child to avoid solving problems.

Customers become aggravated when their questions are answered with the elusive "I don't know." Their impulse is to say, "If you don't know, then find out. I want answers!" The saddest part of this situation is that in most cases employees don't mean to say the wrong thing or provoke frustration. It's just a habit, a slip of the tongue.

It isn't unusual for customers to ask employees questions for which the employees don't know the answers. In fact, this is perfectly normal and is to be expected in most businesses. The point is, *there is no such thing as a question without an answer*. It's the responsibility of employees to provide the best possible service to customers. For this reason, employees must set out to satisfy customers by indicating that their questions will receive the attention they deserve.

Over the years, I have discovered that customers are more interested in *how* their questions are answered than they are in the *content* of the replies. *How* questions are answered tells customers what employees think of them; the *content of the answers* is simply information.

> ## KEY CONCEPT #12
>
> **Every question a customer asks is a request for information that will help the customer make a buying decision, either now or in the future.**

I have found that the best way to answer a customer's question for which you have no answer is to say, "That's a good question. Let me see if I can find out for you."

Always pursue the answers to customers' questions as quickly as possible. Let customers know that they are important to your business and that customer satisfaction is your priority.

If a customer's question requires information that is not readily available to you at the time of the inquiry, take the customer's name and phone number so you can call back with the answer. And always follow up by contacting the customer within a reasonable amount of time. Naturally, this idea of pursuing a customer's satisfaction by a follow-up call will vary with the nature of your business and the nature of the question. Common sense must prevail.

When a customer is shopping at a retail outlet and can't find a specific item, it's a good idea to take the customer to the item. If it's in another department, turn the customer over to the appropriate person in that department when possible. The important thing to remember is that customers must receive the attention they deserve.

Chapter 10

THE CUSTOMER PAYS YOUR WAGES

If I were to ask you, "Who is your boss?" what would your answer be? You would probably tell me the name of your supervisor or manager, right? You would identify the person who makes decisions about how the business is run and gives direction and guidance to the employees. Well, actually, the *customer* fills that description, too.

Not only does the customer tell your business what products, services, and ideas you can sell, but the customer also decides whether your company will grow and prosper and whether there will be a check waiting for you when payday rolls around.

Every dollar you earn comes from the customer's pocket. It may take an indirect route to your own pocket, but if you were to trace its path, the trail would lead you back to the customer. It was the customer's decision to buy that sent your dollar on its way.

Oftentimes employees see the customer as an *outsider*, a person who came in off the street and belongs somewhere else. The fact is, though, that the customer *belongs* in your business, and the more often the better. The customer is the key ingredient to your company's success. The same way a heart is essential to good health because it circulates blood to every vital part of the body, money is the lifeblood of every business, and it's the customer who "pumps" the dollars into the vital parts of your business.

Money is a fascinating subject and is often misunderstood. Most people don't truly understand the process of earning money. The explanation is quite simple. In a free enterprise system, people exchange products and services with one another, but instead of trading, say, a bicycle for a haircut or for the electricity you use, you "trade" money, *which represents the bicycle*. The only value money has is in the products and services it represents. If you couldn't buy products and services with it, it would be worthless. (Incidentally, that's the easiest way to describe *inflation*, too. During inflationary times, money buys fewer products and services than it did previously.)

Most customers feel as though they work hard for their money, and since they have a *limited* supply, they don't want to waste it. They want their money's worth, and if they don't feel as though they're getting it at one business, they'll get it at another. From your own experience, you know that to be true.

Your company needs money in order to pay its light bill, rent, insurance, and the many requirements that keep a business alive, including its most valuable resource, YOU! Good employees, and the way they treat customers, are at the top of the list in all successful businesses. It's a simple matter of economics. Without good employees, businesses would have fewer customers and would starve to death.

KEY CONCEPT #13

Envision yourself asking the customer to sign your paycheck, and you will develop an accurate picture of the customer's place in your own life.

The next time you serve customers, remember that they are making decisions about whether to buy and how much to buy, not just today but tomorrow, too. Treat their purchases with the respect they deserve. After all, those purchases are paying your wages. Everything you currently own was provided by customers. The same is true for everything you will own in the future. The money doesn't come from anywhere else!

Chapter 11

STATE THINGS IN A POSITIVE WAY

When people communicate with one another, they use words to describe the thoughts they hold in their minds. If they choose the correct words, they become successful in creating the same thoughts in the minds of their listeners.

To understand how people communicate, it's important to understand how they think. People think in words, pictures, and feelings. When people are thinking, they are actually saying words to themselves. The words create pictures in their minds. (*For an experiment, try to picture something in your mind without saying the word to yourself first.*)

To illustrate the benefit of positive thinking, I want you to imagine that you have a switch in the middle of your head. The switch is called the PIRRAR switch, and it has only two channels: channel P and channel N.

P stands for *positive*, and N stands for *negative*. The switch doesn't jump back and forth between channels. It rests on either one channel or the other. Unless you are aware of this switch, you might allow elements in the environment to dictate which channel your switch is resting on. That would be a shame, because your thinking travels through this switch, and *thoughts become things*. In other words, the results you achieve in life will be determined by the substance of your thoughts.

KEY CONCEPT #14

Positive thinking produces positive results!

The PIRRAR Switch

PIRRAR is an acronym in which each letter represents an important function of your mental "switch."

The letter P stands for *perceive*. You perceive your environment as being either positive or negative, depending on which channel the switch is resting upon. If the switch is on channel P, life is great! On the other hand, if the switch is on channel N, you have a bleak outlook and negative point of view.

As you go about your daily routine, you tend to see the things you are looking for. For example, if you are in the market to buy a house, you see "For Sale" signs as you drive down any street. The person who is not looking for a house doesn't even see the signs. If you go through life with your switch on channel P, you will see more opportunity and good fortune than the person who is not looking for those things.

So those people who have their PIRRAR switches on channel P see things in a positive way and are optimistic. Channel P thinkers tend to see *problems* as opportunities to succeed, and they realize that every adversity carries the seed of a greater good. They know that there is no such thing as a problem without a solution. They concentrate on solutions, but they realize that some solutions are outside of their control. While recognizing that some customers are "problem people," channel P thinkers accept the fact that they're not in the people-changing business. They do their best and get on with life.

The letter I in PIRRAR represents the word *interpret*. You interpret the messages you get from people and other sources through the PIRRAR switch. You place either a positive meaning on the messages or a negative meaning on them. It depends on where your switch is.

People hear what they need to hear, and anything that can be misunderstood *will be misunderstood*! This is particularly important to remember when dealing with customers. Regardless of what you say to them, they will place their own meaning on your words, depending upon what they *need* to hear. Perhaps you've had experiences in which customers misunderstood you because they needed to hear something else.

As a motivational speaker, I talk to a large number of audiences every year. Every time I speak to a group of people, I realize that everyone in the audience will hear a different message, depending on what he or she needs to hear. I also believe that at least one person in the audience will hear me say something that has profound impact on that person's life. It keeps me humble to realize that what my listeners hear is not always what I mean!

It's important to note that when we communicate with customers, they will not always understand exactly what we mean, even though many times there will be little evidence that this is the case . . . unless things go wrong. When things go wrong (and they will), the positive thinker sees the *problem* as an *opportunity* and takes whatever steps are necessary to create a happy customer.

The first R in the acronym PIRRAR stands for the word *record*. You have billions of cells in the memory portion of your brain. Every experience you've ever had is permanently recorded on those cells. Some of the experiences are easy to recall, while others are more difficult to bring to mind, but they're all residing there as fugitive information.

Your brain is designed as a recording device for two important reasons. The first is so that you develop a growing understanding of the world in which you live. This knowledge is a form of wisdom that helps you succeed in your environment.

The second reason for these recordings is found in the miracle of your imagination and your subconscious mind. Your subconscious mind sorts through all the recordings whenever you have a problem to solve or need some inspiration.

I'm sure you've had the experience of having an idea come to you from "out of the blue" at a time when you were searching for an answer to a problem. This is one reason why goals are so important. When you have a goal, this inspiration-seeking device continually sorts through your past experiences for answers and ideas.

As the positive thinker goes down life's highway, he or she sets the switch on channel P and records life's experiences as positive ones. As a result, information stored in the positive thinker's brain is positive data. When confronted by a problem, the positive thinker will see it as an opportunity and draw the solution from positive ideas. Every positive outcome finds its origin in a positive thought.

When experiences with customers are recorded as being positive, the likelihood of further success is ensured. As opportunities arise to satisfy customers, the positive thinker has lots of great ideas upon which to draw.

The second R in PIRRAR represents two words, *respond internally* (with feelings or emotions). Feelings and emotions are the same thing: mind-and-body responses to the environment. As you encounter something in your environment, the information is processed by your brain and then fed into the hypothalamus, which creates feelings that allow you to respond appropriately.

Feelings are a *readiness to act*. They are neither *good* nor *bad* in the sense of whether or not you should be experiencing them at all. Feelings are natural responses to the environment as it is perceived.

Positive thinkers experience more positive feelings than negative ones, enjoy life more, and meet challenges with enthusiasm.

It's easier for positive thinkers to be successful with customers because they have positive feelings toward those customers. Positive thinkers have the *desire* to create happy customers and see abundant opportunity to do so. There's a natural attraction between positive thinkers and customers.

Feelings are contagious. In the workplace where positive attitudes abound, everyone enjoys life more.

Customers are happier, workers are happier, and the boss is happier.

The A in the acronym PIRRAR stands for the word *act*. Remember that feelings are a readiness to act in response to the environment. After a feeling is acted out it no longer exists, but a feeling will remain if it's not acted out.

Sometimes a person will pick up a feeling in one environment and then act it out in another, like the person who has a bad day at work and later vents the anger at home.

How well employees do at their jobs is generally judged by the sum total of their actions. Whether their actions are positive or negative will determine how employees are perceived both by customers and by employers. The actions of employees will trigger either positive or negative feelings in other people.

The final R in PIRRAR stands for *reap*. You will always *reap the result of your actions*. That's the law that governs the universe—*the law of cause and effect* that for every action there will always be a predictable reaction. As I say in my seminars, "The seed you sow will be the lawn you mow." It's the law.

A large number of people foolishly ignore the law of cause and effect. The world is full of people who are unhappily trying to pound square pegs into round holes. These folks have never stopped to consider trying a new approach.

The law of cause and effect definitely applies to customer relations. If "happy customers" is the desired effect, then the "law" says there must be a *cause* that can make it happen.

Taking this thought a step further, we can be confident it will be a positive cause that brings positive results. The positive thinker must reap positive results; there is no alternative. That brings us back to our first consideration of the PIRRAR switch. People will be successful in life to the extent that they monitor the switch they carry in their heads.

Each of us is gifted with two powers that can affect the quality of our lives. The first is the ability to monitor our thinking, and the second is our power to choose.

When we combine the two powers (ability to monitor our thinking and power to choose), we arrive at a third power: *the power to choose how we think.* And when we take advantage of our ability to control our thinking, we take control of our destiny, because *thoughts become things.* This success secret is not new. It's been around for years: *You become what you think!*

KEY CONCEPT #15

Form the habit of controlling your thinking. Set your own PIRRAR switch to channel P and you will:

- **PERCEIVE your own surroundings in a positive way. You'll recognize opportunities for happiness and success.**

- **INTERPRET the messages you receive from your environment in a positive way. It's good news!**

- **RECORD your experiences as positive ones, and as a result you will build a storehouse of positive information that will help you arrive at constructive decisions and develop positive ideas.**

- **RESPOND INTERNALLY with positive emotions, and you will feel good about life much of the time.**

- **ACT in a positive fashion, and the world will be a better place. You will soon develop the sort of positive charisma that sets you apart from the negative thinkers.**

- **REAP the reward you deserve. Remember, for every positive seed you sow, there will be a positive harvest. It's the law of cause and effect.**

Here is how to apply the philosophy of the PIRRAR switch to the art of positive customer relations. There are three steps that involve activities related to the switch. Place your switch on channel P, and:

1. **Think in positive words.** Remember, you think in words, pictures, and feelings, and *thoughts become things*. Look upon every customer encounter as an opportunity to be happy and successful during your time on the job.

2. **Choose to speak in positive words.** Use your free will and your ability to carefully select positive words when you speak. Your words create pictures in your listener's mind. The pictures can be positive or negative, depending on what you say. Remember, thoughts become things, and from positive thoughts must come positive results!

3. **Hold other people in unconditional positive regard.** Every person is special, just as you are. Some people are more difficult than others, but you must look beyond their lack of perfection and speak to the *good* that is within them. You will soon discover that it blesses your own life when you treat customers and

fellow employees as though they're important. Set a goal for yourself that you will do or say something to the people you encounter that allows them to like themselves better.

BRIGHTEN EVERY CUSTOMER'S DAY

There's a wonderful law that governs customer relations. It's called the *sunshine boomerang law*, and it's a clear example of how the law of cause and effect operates at the human relations level. The sunshine boomerang law simply stated is this: *whenever you brighten another person's life, the result is that you brighten your own!*

KEY CONCEPT #16

The law of cause and effect, as it applies to human relations, guarantees that when one person makes another person happy, the happiness returns to the giver. It's called the sunshine boomerang law.

Customer relations gives each of us an excellent opportunity to brighten our own lives—and at the same time helps our business prosper. Customer relations is clearly a situation of *human relations*. It's a relationship between people. Just think of how much opportunity you have for a happier life yourself by making each customer a happier person! The occasions for your own happiness are almost unlimited.

The world—*your world*—can be a better place if you take the small amount of time required to apply this marvelous principle of happiness. All you need to do is consciously sow the seeds of happiness in every customer you serve. Make it a point to have each customer think, "Gee, I'm glad I spoke to that person."

If you keep this idea in mind as you deal with customers, it will soon become a habit that finds its way into other areas of your life as well. Without realizing it, you will begin to develop the marvelous trait of *personal charisma*. You will begin to stand out as someone special in the eyes of other people.

To prove the sunshine boomerang law to yourself, pause for a moment and call to mind a person who has been very special to you . . . a person who made you feel important and as though you really counted for something. Chances are, it was a person who treated you with great respect. It might have been when you were a child.

The impressions we receive as children are significant to our discussion here. Every grown-up has a *little child* within. Sometimes the little child is hard to see because of the mask of seriousness that many adults wear—but the child is there! I have yet to have an adult deny this when I speak on the topic during a seminar.

The little child in each of us believes what other people say about us, and no matter how well we hide our feelings, the way we are treated by others always penetrates the mask and finds its way to the child. That's why we must never become involved in put-down jokes with other people. When we tease customers, they may be smiling on the outside, but the little child inside of them doesn't like it, and their experience becomes a negative one.

KEY CONCEPT #17

Put-down jokes that are designed to tease or entertain customers are never constructive to business, and they nearly always result in negative experiences for customers.

If you want to use humor with customers, be certain that they are not the brunt of your humor. Other serious things to consider are off-color jokes or stories. Customers might politely laugh at them, but they feel a little less respect for those who tell them. There are lots of other things to talk about.

Chapter 13

ALWAYS GO
THE EXTRA MILE

All the customers who walk into your place of business have some expectations regarding the service they will receive and what will transpire while they are being served by your company. They develop these expectations in their minds as part of deciding to do business with you. It's a natural part of the process each of us uses when deciding upon future activity. Customers whose experiences match their expectations are satisfied, and customers whose experiences fall short of their expectations are dissatisfied.

The secret of top-notch customer relations is to always do just a little more than the customer expects. Surprise your customers by going the extra mile. They will then walk away from your business feeling as though they got more than they bargained for, and it follows logically that they will return to your business to satisfy their needs. They will also give your company the informal sort of endorsement that is such a powerful form of advertising.

KEY CONCEPT #18

Doing just a little more than the customer expects (extra-mile service) is a surefire way to develop customer loyalty.

When businesses discover creative ways to provide a little extra service to customers, they are richly rewarded for the effort. Usually the *little bit extra* requires very little effort or expense, and when measured against all that it takes to keep a business going, it can represent a wise investment in the future.

There's a logical cause-and-effect chain of events that forms a success principle that can be applied to customer relations and can guarantee prosperity in business. This *chain of events* can be visualized as seven dominoes standing on end and lined up in a row. When the first domino is tipped over, it strikes the succeeding domino, which in turn strikes the next, forming a chain reaction that eventually topples all the dominoes.

KEY CONCEPT #19

The seven dominoes for prosperity in business are desire, goal, inspiration, creativity, service, success, and rewards.

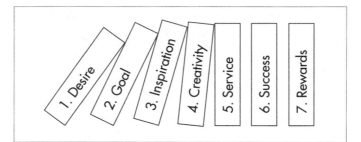

1. **Desire.** Desire is a powerful motivator. When we *desire* to be outstanding in the area of customer relations, the second domino comes into focus.

2. **Goal.** As the result of *desire* for success with customers, we begin to formulate specific goals in our mind about how this desire can be satisfied.

3. **Inspiration.** Any time that we have a *goal* that is laced with *desire*, it activates our own internal success mechanism, our subconscious mind, and as a result we begin to get ideas about how we can reach our *goal*.

4. **Creativity.** Once we begin to get our ideas or inspiration in support of our goal, a marvelous little miracle occurs. The miracle is called *creativity*. Something new exists that did not exist before!

5. **Service.** Creativity is not creativity until it is given away. The object of creativity must be shared with others in such a way that their lives are richer as a result. It must *serve* other people.

6. **Success.** Your business—any business—will be successful only to the extent that it serves other people. The more *service* your business provides to people, the more *successful* it must become.

7. **Rewards.** The law of compensation, which states that for every action there must be a reaction, also states that every act of *service* must be *rewarded*. In our free enterprise system, rewards take the form of money, the method by which we exchange goods and services with each other.

KEY CONCEPT #20

Businesses are not successful because they earn a lot of money. They earn a lot of money because they are successful, and their success is a result of serving customers.

The cause-and-effect pattern outlined above is a logical pathway to success in business, and it can be followed by every company that wants to prosper. It took me quite some time to identify the "seven dominoes of success," but once I made this important discovery, I knew I had a pattern that could be shared with others. In my own experience, I have seen this plan applied with overwhelming success, but there is one important key to remember. Without giving sufficient attention to this key, the formula will not work. The key idea is this: set your desire on *service* rather than rewards, and your success will be guaranteed! The rewards will follow quite naturally.

If you ask yourself these two questions—"Whom can I serve, and how can I serve?"—I feel confident that you will find the answers within your own business. And the answers to these important questions will provide ideas that will lead to the sort of customer relations that can guarantee the prosperity of your company.

"The secret of top-notch customer relations is to always do just a little more than the customer expects."

Part 3

How to Win and Keep More Customers

Chapter 14

THE CUSTOMER SERVICE SCALE

The first step toward improving anything is to *measure* it. Only then can its improvement be determined. It's the same way with customer service.

It took me several years to discover a method for measuring customer service that could be applied to virtually every business. The idea came to me right before a luncheon meeting. I sketched the customer service scale on a paper napkin, and the design has remained the same ever since. The scale has helped a large number of companies improve their business.

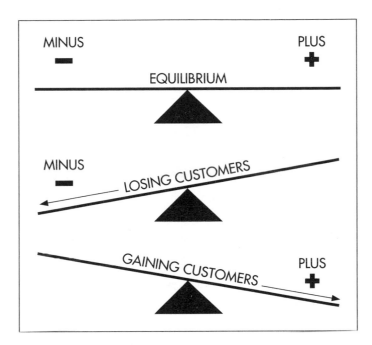

KEY CONCEPT #21

The first step toward improving customer service is to measure the level of service you currently provide and then to determine the level you wish to provide.

As you examine the customer service scale, you will notice that it resembles a teeter-totter. When a company performs on the left side of the scale, it loses more customers than it gains. Companies that want to prosper and grow in the marketplace must consistently perform on the right side of the scale, and the further to the right, the better!

As you become acquainted with the customer service scale, you will notice how simple it is for you to measure your own experience as a customer. The next time you are a customer, it will be easy for you to grade the service you receive.

Let's begin with the center of the scale. I named this equilibrium point *"dial-tone* service" because it's like picking up the telephone and getting the dial tone. No telephone customers get excited about the dial tone: it's what they expect.

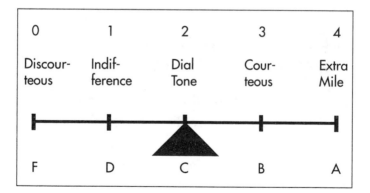

0	1	2	3	4
Discour-teous	Indif-ference	Dial Tone	Cour-teous	Extra Mile
F	D	C	B	A

Many companies operate at the dial-tone level of service. They do just enough to meet customers' expectations. Nothing more, nothing less. These companies trudge along in the marketplace. They get by, but they don't excel.

When customers visit a dial-tone-operating business, they are not distracted by service that is either excellent or awful. They get what they expect, and that's all. We can say customers would give the company a C on its service report card for "average" performance.

Moving toward the left end of the scale, our first stop is "indifference." When customers are met with indifference from employees, they get the impression that the company doesn't care about customers. Customers would give the company a D for poor performance on its service report card.

At the indifference level of operation, a company loses more customers than it gains, unless it happens to be an organization that has no competition, such as the postal service or the Department of Motor Vehicles. Companies in the competitive business environment cannot afford to treat their customers with indifference.

From your own experience as a customer, you can probably think of examples of indifference in a place of business. If so, you can recall that you felt bothered as a customer and were not eager to return.

At the far left end of the scale is "discourteous service," which is characterized by rude behavior on the part of an employee. In the case of discourteous service, the employee goes out of his or her way to offend the customer and, thus, receives a failing grade of F in customer relations.

Companies that perform at the discourteous service level are becoming more scarce. The reason is simple: they're out of business! Given the choice, customers will not accept such service and will take their business elsewhere.

Discourteous service is a *perception* on the part of the customer, and it's the customer's perception that counts. No business would purposely offend its customers, but human nature being what it is, some employees consistently antagonize other people. It might be the employee who needs to be "right" all the time and cannot resist arguing with customers, or it might be the employee who doesn't like other people, including customers.

Winning and Keeping More Customers

The right-hand side of the scale represents the kind of customer care that helps a company succeed in the marketplace. If you and your business consistently operate at the right side of the scale, you can expect to win and keep more customers.

Moving from the middle of the scale, our first stop on the right is "courteous service," which is characterized by customer-focused behavior. Companies that provide courteous service realize that the customer is the only reason for their existence. People in these businesses live by the rule of "customers first, always!"

The best way to provide courteous service is to apply the golden rule to every business encounter by treating *all* customers exactly as you wish to be treated as a customer. Granted, some customers are easier to please than others, but it's the real pro who treats everyone with the same courteous respect. Remember, you treat people the way you do because of who *you* are, not because of who *they* are.

At the far right hand end of the scale, we find "extra-mile service," which is characterized by service that exceeds a customer's expectations. Companies that consistently operate at the extra-mile level almost always excel in the marketplace. These innovative businesses are constantly adding fresh ideas about how to serve customers better, faster, and more fully.

Every company should have monthly "extra-mile meetings" during which employees participate in brainstorming sessions designed to discover new ways to exceed customer expectations. When employees are able to see their own ideas put to work for the benefit of the company, it makes them feel more significant.

Once the floodgates of extra-mile creativity are opened, a steady stream of new ideas continues to flow. It's exciting!

Extra-mile service does not necessarily add additional expense to a company's operating costs, but when it does, the results always outweigh the expenditures.

The Significance of the Customer Service Scale

Consciously or unconsciously, customers are using the same criteria found on the customer service scale to judge the kind of service they receive at every place of business. They are using the criteria to shape their attitudes about your company and whether they want to continue to do business there.

KEY CONCEPT #22

Customers are judging and grading the service they receive during every transaction at your place of business, and at the same time, they are deciding whether or not to return.

From your own experience as a customer, you know how easy it is to judge the kind of service you receive. Your customers are the same way.

You and your company must decide at what level of customer service you want to operate. Then it is simply a matter of deciding what must be done to achieve that level of service. Usually the answers are obvious. The "Ten Commandments for Customer Relations" found in this book are a good starting point for improving service.

Chapter 15

HOW TO HANDLE CUSTOMER COMPLAINTS

It's bound to happen—it's one of the facts of life in business. Occasionally, customers will feel as though they have been mistreated or did not get their money's worth. No matter how diligently a company attempts to conduct its business in a correct fashion, customer complaints will arise from time to time. It would be unfair to suggest that the business is always at fault when customer complaints arise, but the question of *who is at fault* should not be the focus for handling customer complaints.

The tendency in each of us is to "fix the blame." In other words, we tend to become defensive and find creative ways to convince others that it is not our fault when things go wrong. The activity of fixing the blame does little to resolve conflicts in a constructive manner. It is generally recognized as a waste of time.

KEY CONCEPT #23

When handling a customer complaint, the question of who is at fault should never take precedence over resolving the complaint in favor of customer satisfaction.

Customer complaints must be viewed as *opportunities* rather than *problems*. When customers complain about a product or service, it means that they are looking for some form of satisfaction. It's the *opportunity to provide satisfaction* that employees must seek. This positive approach will carry every employee to greater success in handling customer complaints. Look for the opportunity in every complaint!

When customers complain and do not receive the satisfaction they feel they are entitled to, they will generally find satisfaction in other ways. They won't let up until they're satisfied, maybe even looking for a little extra satisfaction for good measure. The "satisfaction" we're talking about here is *negative* satisfaction, and dissatisfied customers can exact it by several means, such as enhancing the story in their favor as they recount their poor treatment when the topic comes up among friends and family, who, incidentally, repeat the story as their contribution to other conversations. Or dissatisfied customers might send nasty letters to the owners of the company, the Better Business Bureau, the letters-to-the-editor column of the local newspaper, or the consumer protection division of the state's attorney general's office, . . . or perhaps post it on the Internet. Let's face it, who needs that kind of negative advertisement!

KEY CONCEPT #24

The complaining customer will find satisfaction one way or another. The smart business makes every attempt to create positive rather than negative satisfaction.

It's not unusual for customer complaints to take an employee by surprise. When this happens, it can be a shocking experience that catches the employee off guard. Every job falls into a routine or pattern after a while, and when this pattern is broken by confrontation with an angry customer, it takes a few moments to shift gears mentally. When confronted by an angry customer, it's important to *respond* rather than react. By *respond*, I mean the employee must take deliberate and measured steps to handle the customer complaint rather than act without thinking.

Customers who return to your place of business to "blow off steam" that has been accumulating prior to their visit have you, as an employee, at a significant disadvantage. These irate customers have been rehearsing exactly what they are going to say, what you will probably say, and how they are going to respond to what you say. It's as though the customers are prepared with a script as they begin to complain. The script generally does not work out exactly the way the customers thought it would, but sometimes they won't pay attention to that fact and will continue to argue long after it is no longer necessary to do so. They just can't seem to let up until they've said it all.

A good way to envision the angry customer is to picture the customer as a balloon blown up to nearly the bursting point. Imagine that when the customer begins to speak, it's as though someone let go of the balloon and let it frantically flit around the room propelled by its compressed contents escaping from its vent. Irate customers are sometimes like that, because you need to let them blow off the pressure before you can deal with them in a constructive manner. And after the pressure is gone, you will discover a change for the better . . . most of the time.

KEY CONCEPT #25

Seven steps for handling customer complaints:

1. **Listen attentively to everything the customer has to say.**
2. **Ask questions that help clarify your understanding of the situation and that let the customer know you are paying serious attention.**
3. **Propose a solution to the problem.**
4. **Make certain the customer will be satisfied with the solution.**
5. **If the solution is unsatisfactory to the customer, ask what solution would be satisfactory.**
6. **If the customer's solution falls within the scope of company policy and you have the authority to grant the solution, it is best to do so as quickly as possible.**
7. **If the customer's solution does not conform to company policy or isn't**

> **within your authority to grant, then explain the situation and take whatever steps are required to at least try to satisfy the customer.**

1. **Listen attentively to everything the customer has to say.** It is important that you look at the customer while he or she is talking to you and that you nod occasionally as you listen to acknowledge that you are following the conversation. Be a good listener, and don't interrupt while the customer is speaking. Give the customer every indication that you are interested in the problem. As you listen, provide plenty of opportunity for the customer to say it all.

2. **Ask questions that help clarify your understanding of the situation and that let the customer know you are paying serious attention.** If you listened carefully to what the customer was saying, you probably picked up a few items in the conversation about which you can ask constructive questions. Not only does asking questions clarify your own understand-

ing and make the customer feel important, but it also draws out the last little bit of steam that might remain. Your questions should be aimed at clarifying the situation and should avoid putting the customer on the defensive.

You will begin to notice a change in most customers as you reach this point in handling their complaints. Usually, customers become ready to deal with their situations constructively once they have vented their anger. They are then ready to do some listening.

Always remember that there is no need for you to take the anger of your customers personally. They really do need someone to talk to, and although they may appear to be directing their anger toward you, it is their *frustration* that is creating the anger. It is not uncommon for young employees to make the mistake of letting irate customers ruin their day by taking personally the things that customers say. As an employee, you are not there to get hurt.

3. **Propose a solution to the problem.** Generally speaking, an obvious solution to the customer's complaint will come to mind as a result of your listening, and it will be a solution that is acceptable to your business and to the customer. Smile and state your solution in a positive manner.

4. **Make certain the customer will be satisfied with the solution.** It is important to seek the customer's buy-in to the solution. Smiling and nodding as you ask for agreement enhances the likelihood of your success. If the customer appears to be satisfied with your solution, act upon it as quickly as possible. Remember, you want to minimize not only the dissatisfaction but also the length of time it exists.

5. **If the solution is unsatisfactory to the customer, ask what solution would be satisfactory.** If the discussion gets this far, you may be surprised at what some people consider fair and equitable. While most people are rational, there are others who think they are entitled to much more than can reasonably be expected by way of redressing the "wrong" that has been inflicted upon them. Some people think that companies have unlimited supplies of money for the purpose of overcompensating the occasional mistake.

   Let's hope that the customer's solution to the problem is reasonable and will serve as a suitable alternative to your own suggestion. This is usually the case, because most people seem to have a sense of what's fair.

6. **If the customer's solution falls within the scope of company policy and you have the**

authority to grant the solution, it is best to do so as quickly as possible. A customer is more likely to be happy when things go his or her way. And when you take this extra step to ensure that the customer is satisfied, you also enhance the likelihood of benefiting by the customer's future business.

7. **If the customer's solution does not conform to company policy or isn't within your authority to grant, then explain the situation and take whatever steps are required to at least try to satisfy the customer.** There will be times when solutions to customer complaints do not come easily, and there will also be times when customer satisfaction can truly tax your creativity. But it is extremely important that every attempt be made to make the customer happy. There really is no such thing as a problem without a solution, but sometimes the solution is outside of your control.

When you run up against a brick wall in your attempt to satisfy the customer's complaint, the best thing to do is be honest and tell the customer that you are perplexed by the situation. Explain that you understand how he or she feels about the situation and how much you wish that you could do something about it. Let the customer know that you care and offer a genuine apology. Sometimes there's not much more you can do than that. The important thing is that you reflect as much kindness as possible. Who knows—the customer may reconsider the situation and return happily in a few days.

Chapter 16

CUSTOMER PET PEEVES AND HOW TO AVOID THEM

All customers have their own special pet peeves when it comes to doing business. Their pet peeves vary in nature and intensity, but every one of them triggers enough frustration and anger to affect their buying decisions.

KEY CONCEPT #26

Customer pet peeves sometimes have their origin in a company's attempt to provide better service or to streamline the operation of the business.

No business sets out to intentionally irritate customers. In fact, many pet peeves begin as ways to serve customers better. For example, many businesses have installed voice mail or department-selection recordings as part of their telephone systems. The idea, of course, is to help customers communicate more efficiently or to get to the right department in a systematic way. In asking members of any audience (customers) how they like these services, at least 85 percent of them register dissatisfaction, ranging from mild irritation to intense disgust.

Here are five things customers don't like, along with the steps you can take to eliminate them from the business place. Remember, the customer's perception is the one that counts! You may have developed a blind spot to some things that have become customer irritants.

1. **Discourteous service.** Discourteous service embodies a long and varied list of negative behaviors experienced by customers. They range all the way from an employee walking into a customer's path rather than giving way to having employees register downright contempt for the customer. More customers are lost by discourteous service than by any other action.

    Treat *every* customer with the same amount of respect you would give to one of your "heroes" if he or she visited your place of business.

2. **Indifference.** When customers get the impression that they don't matter in the eyes of the business or its employees, they depart quickly. The opposite of *indifference* is *caring*. Remember, your business exists for only one reason: the customers! Show customers that you care by focusing on their interests.

3. **Being ignored.** When customers feel as though they are being ignored, they take whatever steps are necessary to remedy the situation. They might take the initiative required to get the attention they deserve, or they might complain, or they might get angry. Whatever action they choose, have no doubt about their getting the attention! Customers won't return to places where they feel invisible.

   Keep your antennae up and be alert when a customer approaches. Give every customer early eye contact and a friendly greeting. Even if you're busy serving another customer, take a moment to meet the new customer's glance with a nod and a friendly smile.

4. **Waiting.** People today are accustomed to "instant everything." They have microwave ovens, instant access to information, fast food, and charge cards. No need to wait!

   "Waiting" is *perception*. When things take longer than people think they should, they feel as though they're waiting. A business should always take steps to make certain the customer has an accurate picture of how long things take. (Don't overpromise.)

5. **Being subordinated to other customers or activities.** When customers feel as though they've been put in second place, it makes them feel unimportant. They don't like to assume second place behind an incoming telephone call, a housekeeping chore, or other customers.

Every business should live by the rule of "Customers first, always!" It's a slogan that's easy to say but often broken.

Things Customers *Do* Like

1. **Customers like to do business with friendly people.** When asked during customer surveys, most people say they return to their favorite places of business because the people are friendly.

2. **Customers like to do business where employees are knowledgeable.** Customers say they feel more confident about the business as well as their purchases when employees have sufficient product knowledge.

3. **Customers like to do business where they get good value for their money.** Today, more than ever before, customers are interested in *quality*. They want and expect durable and functional merchandise.

4. **Customers like to do business where they know they will be treated fairly if a problem arises.** Customers are driven away from companies where they feel at risk.

5. **Customers appreciate places where it's easy to do business.** Customers just love hassle-free transactions. The easier it is to do business, the better they like it.

Chapter 17

CUSTOMER RELATIONS ON THE TELEPHONE

Few businesses could survive without the telephone. The telephone is a company's lifeline to the outside world. Incoming and outgoing calls keep a company in touch with its suppliers, customers, and colleagues. Telephone conversations *are* the next best thing to being there! Using the telephone is the best substitute for visiting the business in person, and how the telephone is used is extremely important to customer relations.

Businesses lose opportunities to serve customers whenever the customers are not handled properly on the telephone. We only have one opportunity to make a first impression, and often it is a telephone conversation that provides that valuable first impression. Customers will make quick decisions about your business based upon their initial telephone contact with it. The business that wisely seeks the opportunity to make customers feel good pays close attention to every telephone call.

Let's begin with some ideas about how to answer the telephone. The most common mistake employees make in answering the phone is in speaking so fast that the customer can't understand what's been said. When the telephone is answered, the employee's total attention must shift to the caller, and the standard greeting must be clear and at an easy-to-understand pace. When the greeting is mechanical and automatic, the customer reads indifference in the voice of the person who answers the telephone and begins to feel as though the business doesn't care.

Have you ever stopped to consider that you can actually *smile* with your voice while you're talking on the telephone? That's right! If you're happy to be talking to the person, your voice will radiate a warm and friendly smile right through the telephone wire. If you do this while speaking to customers, it makes them feel glad they called. It's good for business.

KEY CONCEPT #27

Always smile with your voice while talking to a customer on the telephone.

Incoming calls should be answered as promptly as possible so that the customer is not kept waiting. It is important that the telephone *not* be picked up while the employee is in the middle of a sentence that is part of a conversation with another person. When this happens, the customer feels as though he or she is interrupting, and things get off on the wrong foot.

KEY CONCEPT #28

Always treat a customer's telephone call as if it were a personal visit to your business. Give all callers the courteous attention they deserve.

Sometimes an incoming caller must be put on hold because the person who answered the telephone is handling a caller on another line. Always give incoming callers an opportunity to respond to the question, "Can you please hold for a moment?" rather than cutting them off immediately. Sometimes the incoming caller has a quick question that can be answered in less time than it takes to process a "hold call." If it's necessary to put a customer on hold, always thank the customer for holding. It is best not to have customers wait on the telephone for more than one minute. If it appears as though a customer must wait longer, then come back on the line to inform the customer and ask if it would be more convenient to have the call returned within a few minutes.

When talking to a customer on the telephone, never cover the mouthpiece in order to get involved in a conversation that is not relevant to the caller's interest. The caller always feels subordinated under these circumstances. N*ever* cover the mouthpiece and say something while the customer is talking on the telephone. Generally, the caller can hear and understand whatever is being said, even behind a covered mouthpiece.

Most of what applies to all other aspects of good customer relations also applies to telephone conversations with customers. Keep in mind that every time you talk to a customer, you want to speak in a positive manner, brighten the customer's day, and provide the best possible service. If the customer gives his or her name, it is a good idea to use the name occasionally during the conversation. Calling the customer by name *personalizes* the call and helps give the customer some of the recognition he or she would get by a personal visit to your place of business.

Part 4

Customer Relations Is Human Relations

Chapter 18

UNDERSTANDING HUMAN NATURE

One of the greatest joys in working with the public is in learning to be successful with all kinds of people. This chapter and the next three describe how people differ from one another and explain how you can be successful with various personality types. As we discuss some of these personality types, you will begin to associate some of them with people you already know.

KEY CONCEPT #29

Understanding and working with different types of people can become one of the most enjoyable aspects of any job that involves customer relations.

It's true that no two customers are exactly alike. Every person is unique, but people do fall into patterns of behavior that become easy to identify once you know what to look for. Once you understand what makes people tick, you have the key to becoming more successful with them. The first consideration when determining how to deal effectively with a customer is to make a quick decision about whether the person is an extrovert or an introvert.

Customers who are extroverts are outgoing and like to make their presence known to those around them. They thrive on involvement with other people and enjoy receiving lots of attention. Because extroverts are interested in the world outside themselves and how they affect it, we want to be especially responsive to them. Extroverts may have lots to say and need a good listener. Extroverts often ask many questions to satisfy their curiosity.

Customers who are introverts are quite the opposite of extroverts. Introverts tend to be more private about their thoughts and feelings, and although they need to know that they will get the service they deserve, they don't require as much attention as extroverts. Introverts may have some questions, but the questions will be more thoughtful and designed to help them understand how a product or service meshes with their own *inner world*. Customers with this personality type are often misunderstood because they may appear to be unfriendly and aloof. And because they do not often demonstrate strong enthusiasm, they may seem to be lukewarm buyers. They're different from extroverts in that they're "incoming" rather than "outgoing." Treat introverts in a low-key, friendly manner because they are sizing up you and your business and will make a buying decision that is based on inner thoughts and feelings.

A person cannot be both an extrovert and an introvert at the same time, but a person can lean one way or the other in different situations. You may be surprised to witness the generally introverted customer in a situation in which he or she seems quite outgoing, such as at a family gathering or sporting event.

Every personality is a mixture of introversion and extroversion, although one of the patterns will tend to dominate. It will be more difficult to determine which is the dominant pattern with some customers because they are neither strongly introverted nor strongly extroverted; with these people it is easier to match your approach with their personality because they are comfortable with both patterns.

If our discussion of personality types helps you determine whether you are an extrovert or an introvert, all the better. No matter which type you are, the key to your success with other people is found in acting in a way that is natural to you. You can be a friendly introvert as well as a friendly extrovert, but the important thing to remember in customer relations is *to be friendly*! If you are a new employee, you are likely to be more of an introvert while becoming familiar with your new surroundings. Once you become comfortable and confident in your surroundings, it will be easier to let your personality shine forth!

KEY CONCEPT #30

Customers who are extroverts need strong interaction with employees, while customers who are introverts require a low-key, thoughtful approach that satisfies their inner needs.

"One of the greatest joys in working with the public is in learning to be successful with all kinds of people."

Chapter 19

FOUR CUSTOMER PERSONALITY TYPES

In addition to determining whether a customer is an introvert or an extrovert, we can put each customer into a specific personality-type classification. According to the famous psychologist Carl Jung, every personality falls into one of four basic groups or classifications. Understanding these classifications makes it easier to deal effectively with each customer because personality type is the key to behavior.

According to the theory of personality types, people can be grouped according to these four classifications: *thinkers*, *feelers*, *sensers*, and *intuiters*. As in our discussion of introversion and extroversion, people are generally a mixture of the personality types, but one type will tend to dominate.

1. The Thinker Type

Thinkers are people who are extremely logical and never make up their minds until they believe they have enough information to be confident in the correctness of their decisions. Once they have made up their minds, they are slow to change them. Since thinkers seldom decide quickly, as shoppers they may spend a lot of time looking around before they make purchasing decisions.

You can spot thinkers by observing their behavior. They like lots of information that they can use to make logical and "correct" decisions. They will seriously weigh the benefits of any purchase against the cost of the purchase to make certain of its worth. One clue to the thinker type is that thinkers like to have things in a structured, orderly manner. Thinkers lead structured, orderly lives and get frustrated if their structure and order is upended.

The best way to deal with thinkers is to present your product or service in a logical manner for their consideration. It must make sense to them. Thinkers do not like to be pushed toward or rushed into decisions and will feel uncomfortable if these things happen.

Once thinkers decide to do business with you, they will continue to do so until it makes better sense to take their business elsewhere. Thinkers appreciate consistency in a product's appearance, and they want dependable service.

Roughly 25 percent of all customers are thinkers.

2. The Feeler Type

Feelers are people who make decisions according to their *feelings*. Feelers will decide in favor of things that arouse pleasant rather than unpleasant emotions, beautiful rather than ugly images, and exciting rather than dull experiences. While feelers are quite capable of using logic to make decisions, logic usually takes a backseat to *enjoyment*. Feelers likes colorful items, cozy environments, the latest fads or fashions, and friendly atmospheres for doing business.

You can identify feelers by watching how they act and by listening to what they say. When making decisions, feelers may appear to be a little uncertain until they have the agreement of others rather than risk any *bad feelings* that disagreements can bring. It's not unusual for feelers to change their minds after they make their purchases, because when they take their items home, they have different *feelings* about them. The vocabulary of feelers is usually laced with words that describe things according to feelings.

To be effective with feelers, it's important to present your product or service in a way that arouses pleasant emotions. Feelers love to hear compliments, and being accepted by other people is extremely important to their sense of well-being. Feelers are generally not in a hurry to buy an item until they feel right about it, and they may need a little reassurance from the seller. The seller should emphasize the pleasure that will come from the purchase.

Note: Feelers are generally quite pleasant to have as customers if they receive the attention they deserve, and they also become extremely loyal to their favorite business establishments. But feelers once angered can be hard to get back as customers.

About 25 percent of all people are feelers.

3. The Senser Type

Unlike thinkers and feelers who must ponder decisions in order to sort out logic or to examine feelings, sensers are "right-now" individuals whose minds already seem made up based on the sensory data at hand. Sensers may appear to be impulsive; they do not need to know *why* so much as they need to *act* and get on with things. They're more interested in practicality than they are in logic and beauty.

You can spot senser customers because they're quick to decide and quick to act. If they're shopping for an item, they will give your selection of merchandise a quick examination, choose something that will do the job, pay for it, and leave. And if sensers stand in line to pay for their purchases, they might pick up one or two impulse items that attract them. Sensers do not shop around from store to store for the best deal, because they're simply not interested in making detailed comparisons. With a little imagination you can see how the senser might respond to your own business, no matter what the product or service is.

It's best to use the direct approach with sensers. Give them what they want. The likelihood of being able to "sell" them something is not great. If you think that sensers are making choices that they might become unhappy with later, you can point out the practical aspects of an alternative choice. If these customers *sense* that your observations are correct, they will quickly change their minds and be on their way.

As with all other customers, sensers like courteous service, but they also appreciate service that is quick. Sensers are *convenience* shoppers who will become regular customers if doing business with you is not complicated.

About 40 percent of us are sensers.

4. The Intuiter Type

Like sensers, intuiters are quick to make up their minds and may appear to be impulsive. Intuiters do not ponder decisions, but instead act upon "hunch" or intuition. Intuiters seem to have an inborn sense about things and do not need to gather much information in order to make decisions. Intuiters are often futuristic and creative and usually have fairly accurate notions about "what's coming next."

As customers, intuiters will be the most challenging type to figure out. There's very little about the behavior of intuiters that can tip you off to their type. Intuiters do not like to get bogged down with detail and may tend to be a little disorganized. Because intuiters are often future-oriented, they are interested in whatever is new and different. Customers of this type are less likely to fall into rigid behavior patterns such as going to the same restaurant or developing a strong loyalty to any one place of business.

The best way to handle intuiters is to listen carefully to what they want and to present them with whatever products and services match their vision. You may also wish to point out products and services that will be in demand in the near future. Ask the intuiter lots of questions. You'll be surprised what you can learn!

About 10 percent of us are intuiters.

Important: Each of us is a mixture of the four personality types discussed here, but in most of us one of the types dominates. It should be noted that each of the types has its strengths and weaknesses and that none of the types is either good or bad.

KEY CONCEPT #31

There are four basic personality types: thinkers, feelers, sensers, and intuiters. In the role of customer, each type is distinctly different from the others.

Chapter 20

THREE ROLES CUSTOMERS PLAY

It's been said that life is a stage and each of us selects a role to play. Students of human nature identify three basic roles that people play, especially during times of conflict. Your understanding of these roles and their relationship to one another will be helpful in handling customer complaints and in dealing effectively with difficult people. In a nutshell, the three roles are the *persecutor*, the *victim*, and the *rescuer*.

I'd like to have you stop and think about a drama that really held your interest. It could be a movie, a television show, or a good book. In each case it would be quite easy to assign each of the roles—persecutor, victim, rescuer—to various players in the cast. And it was the way in which these roles *changed* that held your interest and provided the sense of drama that entertained you. Subconsciously, you had a "happy ending" in mind for the drama, which involved the roles shifting to where you wanted them to be. You wanted the persecutor to finally become the victim, the victim to experience justice, and the rescuer to be successful in his or her efforts.

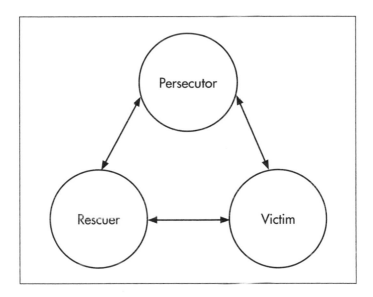

KEY CONCEPT #32

The three basic dramatic roles customers play during times of conflict are persecutor, victim, and rescuer.

1. The Persecutor

We understand the word *persecute* to mean "to oppress or harass another person." People sometimes appear to have a need to persecute others, and they look for opportunities to do so. In order to find such opportunities, it's sometimes necessary for them to develop situations whereby they can become persecutors. Because, in these cases, the act of persecution is based on psychological need, it is often hard to understand why they are so upset over seemingly trivial matters. People who need to persecute want to manipulate others into the victim role.

The manipulative persecutor might be the customer who becomes quite angry if he or she believes that service is too slow, or the customer who makes a scene in a restaurant because there was a mistake in the order, or the customer who purchases a defective item and wants to have a letter about your "lousy merchandise" published in the local newspaper.

Let's face it: some people just seem to need to pick on others. Usually it's because they've had a bad day and things aren't going right for them. As a result, persecutors look for someone to dump on.

The best way to handle persecutors is to recognize them as such and to refuse to assume the victim role to the extent of having it affect your feelings about yourself and your job. Remember, the persecutor is a "problem looking for someplace to happen." Do what you can to satisfy persecutors, but don't take their hostility personally. Let their harsh words roll off like water on a duck's back. Deal with them in a direct and courteous manner, but don't be "sticky sweet" or you will irritate them further.

2. The Victim

In the drama of customer dissatisfaction, the role of *victim* can often enter the picture. Ordinarily we understand the word *victim* to mean "one who was subjected to suffering."

It's interesting to note that some people actually choose the victim role as their favorite role in life. They look for opportunities to be victimized. In order to succeed at becoming a victim, it's sometimes necessary for the player to manipulate another person or group of people into the *persecutor* role. Remember, people who play this role *need* to be a victim, and they are looking for opportunities to fill their need. These folks can cleverly create situations in which they are allowed to "suffer" because of another person's actions.

In addition to manipulating other people into the *persecutor* role, the illegitimate victim may also wish to put people into the *rescuer* role. The roles we are discussing here—persecutor, victim, and rescuer—are based on psychological needs that the players have, and the victim might be starving for attention.

As customers, victims actually like to be in situations in which they get to suffer a bit. When the need arises, they will create situations in which they get to fill that need. Such a situation might involve the person who is careless in selecting shoe sizes or styles and gets to bring the shoes back to the shoe store later. Another situation could be one where the person gets to "suffer through" a steak dinner in which the meat was not cooked as he or she wished. As you picture these situations in your mind, you can begin to see the drama unfold as the victim manipulates another person into the persecutor or rescuer role.

Sometimes the *victim* switches roles to *persecutor* or *rescuer* as the drama unfolds. You will recall from our earlier discussion that it's in the changing of these roles that the actual drama occurs. The victim customer may wish to become the persecutor and to then manipulate the employee into the victim role.

The best way to handle customers who appear to be playing the victim role is to give them plenty of attention and to apologize profusely. As a salesperson, you may wonder how these customers could have gotten themselves into situations containing so much unnecessary discomfort, but you must remember that for some unknown reason they *needed* to do so. Such customers are blind to the pattern of their behavior. Do what you can to satisfy these customers and take steps to make certain the customers do not victimize themselves again at your expense.

If the victim customer wants you to play the role of persecutor or to become the victim, it's wise to "stand outside the drama" and handle the situation in a *professional* manner without getting your personal feelings involved.

3. The Rescuer

The third, and most subtle of the dramatic roles, is that of *rescuer*. The rescuer role is played by people who need to be needed. In customer relations the rescuer role is played more often by employees than by customers, simply by the nature of business. People who *need* to play rescuer work at creating situations in which they get to come to the aid of other people. They find satisfaction in having other people depend upon them.

As customers, rescuers will want to give you some assistance wherever possible. They may offer unsolicited recommendations for improving your business. Rescuers are often sensitive individuals who can get their feelings hurt as the tables turn and they switch to the victim role and say, "All I was trying to do was help."

Rescuer customers can be a source of enjoyment, provided they do not get in the way and become obstacles. Here again, it's wise to give rescuers the attention they crave, but beware of their tendency to move to the victim role for a different type of gratification.

Chapter 21

HOW CUSTOMERS VIEW THEMSELVES

A customer's self-image is an especially important consideration when it comes to customer relations. It can be said that a customer holds one of four basic points of view regarding relationships to other people. It's the *relative* point of view that sets the tone of the *relationship* between you and your customer, and it's determined by a feeling of what we'll call "OK-ness."

KEY CONCEPT #33

The four basic life positions that customers hold in relationship to other people are:
1. I'm Not OK—You're OK
2. I'm Not OK—You're Not OK
3. I'm OK—You're Not OK
4. I'm OK—You're OK

For the sake of our discussion, we'll use the word OK-*ness* to mean feelings of confidence and self-acceptance. "OK" people like themselves and feel comfortable with who they are. They are satisfied with being themselves even though they realize they are not perfect.

1. I'm Not OK—You're OK

This position in life is often referred to as the *inferiority complex position*; it stems from the belief by people that their own worth is somewhat inferior to the worth of others. These people believe that their attitudes, ideas, opinions, and behavior must be shaped to gain the acceptance of other people. They base their image of themselves on the smiles and frowns of other people. If people are smiling at them, they're OK; if people are frowning at them, they'd better shape up and adjust their behavior to gain other people's approval.

It should be noted that we all occupy the inferior position during early childhood—perhaps for the first two years. During these two years, we do not understand the meanings of words, we're incapable of logic, we're small in size, and we generally rely on other people to come to our rescue when things go wrong. As infants, we enjoy feeling OK, but we rely on the "big people" to help us feel OK. They become a necessary source of our OK-ness. In fact, that's how they train us: If we want to feel OK, we do what we're supposed to do. If we do something we're not supposed to do, the "big people" take away our OK feelings. So, early in life we gauge our personal success on the smiles and frowns of other people . . . it's inescapable.

Some grown-ups never escape their feelings of inferiority, and often these same people are your customers. You can frequently spot them by the way they act. They may be the braggarts who need to impress people during every conversation, or they may be the ones who are dressed sloppily in order to advertise their inferiority.

The best way to handle customers who have an inferiority complex is to go out of your way to make them feel good about who they are by complimenting them with sincerity and by demonstrating respect. Bear in mind that people who have an inferiority complex feel miserable if they think their behavior is not winning the approval of other people. Because these customers seek approval, they will return to places of business where they feel OK. Go out of your way to make them feel important even when they're bragging or acting in an inferior way.

2. I'm Not OK—You're Not OK

These people can be said to occupy the *cynical life position*. They don't like themselves, nor do they like other people. They developed this attitude early in life when they began doing a few things for themselves and started to understand the meaning of words . . . *if* they had the type of parents who did not demonstrate much affection toward them *and* who were always instilling them with bad feelings in an attempt to get them to do what they were supposed to do. Early in life these people made the decision, "I know I'm not OK, but you aren't too nice either!" Some people grow into adulthood occupying this I'm Not OK—You're Not OK life position.

It's easy to spot customers who have adopted the I'm Not OK—You're Not OK life script. They are the people who are negative about everything. They tend to complain every time they speak, and they seldom trust people with whom they are doing business.

The key to effectiveness with cynical customers is to not let them affect your behavior and the feelings you have about yourself. There is very little you can do or say to change these people's attitudes about themselves and other people, except to provide them with excellent service that is prompt and courteous. If enough people treat these customers this way, their inescapable decision will someday be, "I guess some people are OK."

It should be noted that there are two parts in each of the life scripts we're discussing here. The first part belongs to the people themselves, and the second part belongs (from these people's own point of view) to virtually everyone else they encounter. The person who occupies the cynical position is often capable of projecting the Not-OK part of the script onto the person with whom he or she is speaking, especially toward a young person who has fresh recollections of the adult-child relationships of the recent past. It's a good idea to make an extra effort to refuse ownership of these Not-OK feelings about yourself. Do your best at all times and be assured that you alone are the one who decides your self-worth.

3. I'm OK—You're Not OK

This is said to be the *criminal* position because the folks who occupy it have very little regard for other people. Holders of the criminal position usually come from family situations in which they were abused as children. As youngsters, they already occupied the I'm

Not OK—You're Not OK position as described above, but then later they decided that if they were going to survive in their world, they had better look out for "number one," themselves. They grew into adulthood as the type of selfish person who has very little respect for other people.

As customers, I'm OK—You're Not OK people will be nice to you as long as there's a direct payoff for doing so. When the payoff is no longer likely, they shift their attention to other situations that can show promise for enhancing their lives. These customers are usually easy enough to do business with, provided they receive excellent service and *always* feel as though they are given favored treatment that others do not receive. If they feel as though they have been neglected customers, they are quick to set friendship and loyalty aside and do whatever is necessary to receive their own satisfaction.

It's especially important for you to treat I'm OK—You're Not OK customers with extra kindness. These customers have few—if any—friends and have little opportunity to experience the joy of loving relationships. The world becomes a better place when these people are treated with compassion, and you and your business will have one more reason to be proud of yourselves when you overlook the blemish on this type of personality.

One word of caution: I'm OK—You're Not OK people generally believe that they are right and you are wrong if there's a disagreement between them and you, and they will act as though there is no question about their correctness. Agree with them where you can, try to keep them satisfied, and go on about your business. Don't let their incorrect attitudes ruin your day.

4. I'm OK—You're OK

This is considered to be the *healthy* position in life. It's the foundation for all success in customer relations. People who accept this life position as a basic life script recognize their own personal worth as well as the worth of others. They know they aren't perfect, but they've grown to accept themselves as they are. They try to do well in whatever they attempt because they have respect. They see other people as being very much like themselves, and so they accept them, too.

Those who occupy this healthy I'm OK—You're OK life position have made a decision about themselves and other people. The decision goes something like this: "The only person I can ever be is myself. I guess I'm as OK as anyone is, so I may as well be a friend to myself and do what I can to have a happy life!" This person also wants other people to experience the joy and peace of mind that comes with such a decision, and treats them with the kind of respect that provides encouragement.

As customers, the people who occupy the I'm OK—You're OK position are a delight to work with. They don't get upset over small matters, and they realize that everyone makes mistakes occasionally. If they have a problem with your product or service, they are quick to understand how those things happen. They're more interested in resolving the problem in a quick and friendly manner. They want to be fair, and they expect to be treated with respect.

Employees who occupy the I'm OK—You're OK position are valuable assets to their employers as well as to customers. It's easy for these employees to be service-oriented and to give customers the kind of attention they deserve.

The positive and healthy self-image of a company's employees can do more to ensure the success of a business than virtually any other asset. If we were to list the benefits associated with positive employee self-images, it could fill a volume titled *How to Succeed in a Customer-Oriented Business*!

KEY CONCEPT #34

The foundation for all successful customer relations is in the I'm OK—You're OK attitude toward people.

Part 5

Basic Selling Skills

Chapter 22

SELLING MAKES THE JOB MORE FUN

If you're like most people, you tend to think of *selling* as a highly specialized skill. Well, you're right . . . up to a point; but the fact is, you've been *selling* since before you can remember. A good, workable definition for the word *selling* is "influencing a decision." In the case of business transactions, the salesperson is influencing the prospect's decision about whether and what to buy. At home, the two-year-old is trying to influence a parent's decision about how much attention the child should receive.

KEY CONCEPT #35

Selling is a skill we all use . . . whether we're in business or not!

You are fortunate indeed if your job provides the opportunity for you to sell. Selling adds zest and interest to any job and thus makes the work more rewarding. When employees are reluctant to sell, it's usually for one of the following reasons:

1. Misconceptions about selling
2. Lack of skill training
3. Fear of rejection

Items 2 and 3 in the list, *skill training* and *handling rejection*, are discussed in the next chapter. In this chapter we focus our attention on misconceptions.

Misconceptions About Selling

Misconception #1: A *person is either a "born salesperson" or not.*
Truth: Selling is a skill, not a personality trait. Salespeople are *trained*, not "born."

Misconception #2: *Selling is for fast talkers.*
Truth: Salespeople sell more by listening than they do by talking. They listen for clues that indicate what customers need or want.

Misconception #3: *Salespeople need to be pushy.*
Truth: Pushy salespeople irritate customers. Consequently they sell less and have virtually no repeat business.

Misconception #4: *Making the sale is the main thing.*
Truth: Helping customers is the main thing. Every business depends on satisfied customers for long-term success.

Misconception #5: *Selling requires occasional dishonesty.*
Truth: Selling requires complete and uncompromising honesty. A single dishonest or untruthful incident can ruin a company's chances for future success.

Misconception #6: *Salespeople are somewhat manipulative.*
Truth: Customers must feel free to decide whether or not to buy. When customers feel manipulated into making decisions, it creates more problems than profit for the company in returned merchandise and loss of future business.

The Buying Decision

The best way for you to understand how customers make their buying decisions is to examine your own experiences as a customer. Let's say you're deciding whether or not to buy a pair of socks. If you'd rather have the socks than the money, then you buy; but if you'd rather have the money than the socks, it's "no sale."

As the illustration below shows, the buying decision is characterized as a teeter-totter scale, with the product (or service) on one side and the dollar amount on the other. The dynamics of the buying decision are illustrated by which side (the product or the money) is more important to the customer.

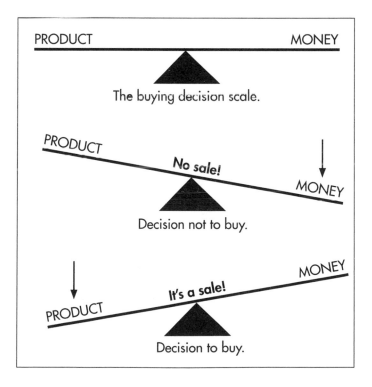

PRODUCT   MONEY

The buying decision scale.

PRODUCT   No sale!   MONEY

Decision not to buy.

MONEY   It's a sale!   PRODUCT

Decision to buy.

KEY CONCEPT #36

Selling is especially easy for the salesperson who wants the customer to profit by every purchase.

It's the salesperson's job to help the customer understand the value of the item and thereby influence the buying decision. The customer's *perception* of the product determines its value in the marketplace. (The company can determine the price, but it's the customer who determines the value.) The successful salesperson finds ways to *add value* to the product in the eyes of the customer, and this is one challenge of selling that makes it so much fun.

THE ABCs OF
SUCCESSFUL SELLING

Selling should be seen as a logical *process* that has a beginning, a middle, and an end. When salespeople understand the process and consciously keep "the horse before the cart," they consistently add to their success.

KEY CONCEPT #37

The five steps in the selling process are:
1. **Rapport**
2. **Interest**
3. **Conviction**
4. **Desire**
5. **Close**

---

1. Rapport

In selling, the term *rapport* means establishing a congenial relationship with the customer. The congeniality must be sincere and must be founded on the idea that the salesperson is there to help the customer.

All of us have had the experience of being greeted by a salesperson who was "too congenial." That kind of aggressive friendliness makes customers wary. It scares them away.

You should establish rapport with customers by greeting them in a well-mannered method that is appropriate to their age and station in life. Use common sense. Ask yourself, "How do I think this customer would prefer to be greeted?" Learn to "read" customers and to approach them on *their* terms. The main thing to remember is to be polite and remain focused on making customers feel at ease.

2. Interest

As the selling process unfolds, it begins with your learning why the customer has come to your place of business. (This step varies, of course, with each business and with your particular circumstance—

depending on whether you are the one who is calling on the customers.) If customers are "just looking," fine, let them look. If appropriate, visit with them while they're browsing. As they depart, don't forget to thank them for visiting your place of business.

For customers who come to your place of business to make a purchase, it's your job to learn what prompted the visit and then to match the customers' needs with the appropriate product. In other words, the interest of customers must be married to the items you have to sell.

In some cases it will be necessary for you to generate some interest in your product by demonstrating its benefits to customers. If your product carries an obvious benefit, customers will pick up on it quickly.

3. Conviction

Once customers are interested in your product, it's your job to assure them that the product will meet their expectations. This can be accomplished by demonstrating the product or by handling any concerns (objections) customers might have regarding it.

One of the most powerful sales tools is the *demonstration*. If you can demonstrate your product to the customer in a convincing way, it will be much easier for you to make the sale. Showing is much more effective than talking. Seeing is believing!

Occasionally, customers have concerns that you must overcome before you can make the sale. Usually, customers raise concerns or objections only if they're thinking about buying. Concerns might be about financing, guarantees, price, quality, or other things. During the *conviction* step of the selling process, the salesperson overcomes the customer concerns by eliminating them.

4. Desire

Most buying decisions are made at the emotional level rather than the logical level. Buyers do what they *feel* like doing. They use logic to support their decisions.

This fact can be validated by examining your own buying behavior. Consider the last time you purchased an automobile. How much of your decision to buy was influenced by *desire* and how much by *logic*? Anytime you experience desire, you are drawn toward the object that triggered the desire.

When the customer sufficiently desires a product, we can say "the sale has been made." If a salesperson tries to close the sale before the customer's desire has peaked, then the salesperson is being pushy in the eyes of the customer. Wait until you believe the customer wants the item sufficiently before you ask for the sale.

5. Closing the Sale

If the customer doesn't say, "I'll take it," it's the salesperson's job to ask for the sale. A large number of sales are lost because salespeople don't ask customers to buy.

When a salesperson doesn't ask for the sale, it's usually out of fear that the customer might say no. Such a salesperson would incorrectly interpret the no as a personal rejection. Fear of rejection is a feeling that all salespeople must overcome.

It would be foolish to assume that every prospect is a buyer. Some prospects buy, while others don't. It's that simple. If six out of ten prospects buy, then every prospect who says no brings the salesperson closer to the one who will say yes. Smart salespeople play it by the numbers. They never take it personally when a prospect says no.

Here's why it's important to ask for the sale. Let's say that one out of twenty customers needs to be asked to buy. That's 5 percent of the customers. If all customers are not asked to buy, then the company loses 5 percent of its business . . . and an even greater amount of profit because the fixed costs associated with operating a business remain the same. (Each additional sale a company makes is more profitable than the one that preceded it.)

Make a game of learning to sell. Constantly add to your skills and techniques. Remember, when it comes to selling, no one can do it *your way* better than you! Follow the pattern outlined above and give each of the steps your own personal touch. It'll give you an opportunity to develop some of your personality traits.

Chapter 24

UPSELLING AND CROSS-SELLING

One of the most satisfying skills an employee can develop is that of upselling a company's products or services. *Upselling* means to move customers up the scale in the value of their purchases. For example, a guest who registers at a hotel might be *upsold* to a better room, or a customer who places an order with a florist might be *upsold* to a more beautiful floral arrangement.

When customers are upsold to better and more desirable products or services, it becomes a win-win situation. The customers come out ahead because they receive something better for a fractional increase in the original price.

KEY CONCEPT #38

The customer who is upsold to a better product or service will generally be happier with the purchase.

The company providing the product or service comes out ahead in a more dramatic way. Here's why: regardless of the dollar amount of all sales, the company must still pay the same *fixed costs*. Fixed costs are those costs associated with being in business, for example, rent, wages, insurance, and electricity. These costs are paid from the gross profit generated from all sales. When an employee upsells to a customer, the additional profit can be seen as "extra" profit because it represents money the company would not otherwise have.

Employees who focus on upselling are extremely valuable to any company and to the success of the business. Every company should have a spectrum of product values and should focus on training its employees to upsell.

A word of caution! We must make a clear distinction between *upselling* and the unsavory practice called *bait and switch*. Bait and switch occurs when a company of questionable integrity advertises a product or service at a low price with the intention of selling something more expensive. Occasionally the bait and switchers claim to have depleted their supply of the advertised product or service. At any rate, their intent is to sell something that is much more expensive than what was advertised.

People who practice bait and switch are usually guilty of other questionable practices, including the way they treat their employees. You would be well advised to avoid working for such a company. Save your loyalty for a firm that practices integrity in the marketplace.

How to Upsell

Upselling occurs only after a customer has decided to purchase a product or service. The initial sale has already been made.

Put yourself in the customer's shoes by thinking of the product or service from the vantage point of the customer. Ask yourself, "What can I suggest to this customer that might add to his or her satisfaction?" It's much easier to *sell with enthusiasm* when you're genuinely interested in the satisfaction of the customer. Often a customer can actually *save money* by spending more. For example, if a customer is purchasing a pair of dress shoes, it's easy for you to be enthusiastic about recommending a more durable pair that will look good for a longer period of time.

The best way to upsell customers is by letting them make the comparison between what they have decided to purchase and an upgraded version. Naturally, when price is a consideration, the difference in quality should be obvious. (My definition of *quality* is "satisfaction that matches price.") When quality is less obvious, it should be explained.

Don't feel as though you are being manipulative by upselling a customer. Upselling should always result in increased customer satisfaction.

KEY CONCEPT #39

The salesperson who forgets to upsell does the customer a disservice.

Cross-Selling

Cross-selling is sometimes referred to as *companion selling*. It occurs when the salesperson recommends an additional item to the customer who has already made a purchase. For example, if a customer buys a hamburger, the salesperson might suggest french fries or a beverage to accompany the purchase.

Virtually every product or service can be married to a companion item. It's the company's job to consider companion items when developing its product line, and it's the job of the salesperson to remember to suggest the companion items to the customer.

Employees who fail to recommend companion items actually perform a disservice to customers. From your own experience as a customer, you know of the times you've made a purchase and forgotten to buy a companion item. For instance, have you ever mailed a package and forgotten to purchase stamps while you were at the post office? Wouldn't you have felt better served if the postal clerk asked, "Do you need any stamps today?" Probably so.

KEY CONCEPT #40

The employee who consistently cross-sells provides a valuable service to the company and the customer.

Always be thinking of how customers might add to their satisfaction or convenience by making companion purchases. Remember, you are doing the customer a favor by mentioning companion items. You are also doing a favor for your employer. The salesperson who consistently recommends companion items to customers makes a significant contribution to the profitability of the company and is therefore a valued employee.

Chapter 25

TEN COMMANDMENTS FOR SUCCESSFUL SELLING

Every salesperson should have a list of basic selling principles from which to operate. By occasionally reviewing the list, the salesperson is more apt to stay focused and to maintain a system of habits that bring success. Here is the checklist I recommend:

1. **Always remember, people buy from people they like!** Take time to make friends with your prospect. Establish a level of rapport that will help you communicate effectively with the customer.

2. **Know your products.** School is never out for the professional salesperson. You must add to your knowledge every day by learning more about your products and how they can help people.

3. **Be proud of your products.** Remember, your products were designed with one purpose in mind: *to help people*. Be proud of that fact and recognize that the more you *sell*, the more you *help*!

4. **Be a good listener.** When you listen to customers, it lets them know you care, and it helps you learn how you can be of service.

5. **Let customers decide.** Don't impose your own tastes, values, or economic circumstances on the right of customers to make their own decisions.

6. **Choose positively.** Positive words create positive pictures in the minds of customers, and since thoughts become things, you can expect more positive results.

7. **Selling is a process, not an event.** The selling process has a beginning, a middle, and an end (rapport, interest, conviction, desire, close). Don't try to take shortcuts or to rush the sequence.

8. **Customers must profit.** Always think in terms of how customers will come out ahead by buying your product or service. Add value to your offerings in the eyes of customers.

9. **Be persistent, but not pushy.** If you're convinced your product is the answer to

customers' needs, be persistent in a friendly way. Find out why customers are saying no and then handle their concerns.

10. **Be philosophical about rejections.** A certain percentage of prospects will buy; a certain percentage won't. That's the way it is. Every no brings you closer to yes.

A final note: Make a game of selling. It can be great fun, and it's especially rewarding as your skills improve.

Part 6

Key Concept Review

Chapter 26

KEY CONCEPTS

1. You as an employee are one of your company's most valuable assets.

2. Use your own experience as a customer to help you understand the principles of good customer relations.

3. The three legs of customer relations are:

   a. The relationship that exists between the employee and the customer

   b. The relationship that exists between the employee and fellow employees

   c. The self-image of the employee

4. In the long run, repeat business depends upon customer satisfaction.

5. Attitudes that help you get ahead:
   a. Think like the boss.
   b. Be a problem finder.
   c. Be 100 percent loyal.
   d. Be enthusiastic!
   e. Do more than you get paid for.
   f. Fix the problem, not the blame.
   g. Don't talk about people.
   h. Be 100 percent honest.

6. There is never a "wrong" time to serve a customer if your doors are open for business.

7. When smiling at a customer, put the look of "I like you!" in your eyes. The rest of your face will then fall into place naturally.

8. People must feel comfortable when doing business with you. Adapt to their style as best you can. Be alert and flexible in your approach to customers.

9. The four rules for remembering names are:
   a. You must *desire* to remember names.
   b. You must *learn* the names you want to remember.
   c. You must *repeat* the names you want to remember.
   d. You must *associate* names with something.

10. Develop the feeling of ownership for your job. It is your life while you are at work. Make the most of it. You will be happy and successful as a result.

11. Two things to remember when handling a customer complaint: handle the complaint quickly so the customer is dissatisfied for the shortest possible length of time, and don't do anything that will add to the customer's dissatisfaction.

12. Every question a customer asks is a request for information that will help the customer make a buying decision, either now or in the future.

13. Envision yourself asking the customer to sign your paycheck, and you will develop an accurate picture of the customer's place in your own life.

14. Positive thinking produces positive results!

15. Form the habit of controlling your thinking. Set your own PIRRAR switch to channel P and you will:

   • PERCEIVE your own surroundings in a positive way. You'll recognize opportunities for happiness and success.

   • INTERPRET the messages you receive from your environment in a positive way. It's good news!

- RECORD your experiences as positive ones, and as a result you will build a storehouse of positive information that will help you arrive at constructive decisions and develop positive ideas.
- RESPOND INTERNALLY with positive emotions, and you will feel good about life much of the time.
- ACT in a positive fashion, and the world will be a better place. You will soon develop the sort of positive charisma that sets you apart from the negative thinkers.
- REAP the reward you deserve. Remember, for every positive seed you sow, there will be a positive harvest It's the law of cause and effect.

16. The law of cause and effect, as it applies to human relations, guarantees that when one person makes another person happy, the happiness returns to the giver. It's called the sunshine boomerang law.

17. Put-down jokes that are designed to tease or entertain customers are never constructive to business, and they nearly always result in negative experiences for customers.

18. Doing just a little more than the customer expects (extra-mile service) is a surefire way to develop customer loyalty.

19. The seven dominoes for prosperity in business are desire, goal, inspiration, creativity, service, success, and rewards.

20. Businesses are not successful because they earn a lot of money. They earn a lot of money because they are successful, and their success is a result of serving customers.

21. The first step toward improving customer service is to measure the level of service you currently provide and then to determine the level you wish to provide.

22. Customers are judging and grading the service they receive during every transaction at your place of business, and at the same time, they are deciding whether or not to return.

23. When handling a customer complaint, the question of who is at fault should never take precedence over resolving the complaint in favor of customer satisfaction.

24. The complaining customer will find satisfaction one way or another. The smart business makes every attempt to create positive rather than negative satisfaction.

25. Seven steps for handling customer complaints:
   a. Listen attentively to everything the customer has to say.

b. Ask questions that help clarify your understanding of the situation and that let the
customer know you are paying serious
attention.

c. Propose a solution to the problem.

d. Make certain the customer will be satisfied
with the solution.

e. If the solution is unsatisfactory to the
customer, ask what solution would be
satisfactory.

f. If the customer's solution falls within the
scope of company policy and you have the
authority to grant the solution, it is best to
do so as quickly as possible.

g. If the customer's solution does not conform
to company policy or isn't within your authority to grant, then explain the situation
and take whatever steps are required to at
least try to satisfy the customer.

26. Customer pet peeves sometimes have their
origin in a company's attempt to provide
better service or to streamline the operation
of the business.

27. Always smile with your voice while talking to
a customer on the telephone.

28. Always treat a customer's telephone call as if it were a personal visit to your business. Give all callers the courteous attention they deserve.

29. Understanding and working with different types of people can become one of the most enjoyable aspects of any job that involves customer relations.

30. Customers who are extroverts need strong interaction with employees, while customers who are introverts require a low-key, thoughtful approach that satisfies their inner needs.

31. There are four basic personality types: thinkers, feelers, sensers, and intuiters. In the role of customer, each type is distinctly different from the others.

32. The three basic dramatic roles customers play during times of conflict are persecutor, victim, and rescuer.

33. The four basic life positions that customers hold in relationship to other people are:
   a. I'm Not OK—You're OK
   b. I'm Not OK—You're Not OK
   c. I'm OK—You're Not OK
   d. I'm OK—You're OK

34. The foundation for all successful customer relations is in the I'm OK—You're OK attitude toward people.

35. Selling is a skill we all use . . . whether we're in business or not!

36. Selling is especially easy for the salesperson who wants the customer to profit by every purchase.

37. The five steps in the selling process are:

    a. Rapport

    b. Interest

    c. Conviction

    d. Desire

    e. Close

38. The customer who is upsold to a better product will generally be happier with the purchase.

39. The salesperson who forgets to upsell does the customer a disservice.

40. The employee who consistently cross-sells provides a valuable service to the company and the customer.

INDEX

Subconscious mind, 86
Success:
    in cause and effect chain of
        events, 103
    seven dominos of, 101–104
Sunshine boomerang law, 33, 94,
    95–96

T
Talking about others, 28
Telephone, 137–141
    covering mouthpiece of, 141
    customer attitudes toward
        automated services, 133
    first impressions and,
        138–139
    follow-up calls, 74
    importance of, 138
    incoming calls on hold,
        140–141
    positive attitude and, 139,
        141
    wait time and, 134–135,
        140–141
Ten commandments:
    for customer relations,
        31–105

for successful selling,
    201–204
Thinker personality type, 152,
    153–154
Trust, of customers, 15–16, 25,
    62–63, 135

U
Unconditional positive regard,
    91–92
Upselling, 194–197
    bait and switch versus,
        195–196
    defined, 194
    importance of, 194–195
    techniques used in, 196–197

V
Victim role, 160–161, 162,
    163–164
Visualization, in remembering
    names, 56–57
Voice mail, customer attitudes
    toward, 133

W
Wait time, 134–135, 140–141

ABOUT THE AUTHOR

Frank Cooper is one of America's most popular speakers. He is the author of *How to Grow a Profitable Business* and is featured on numerous audio and video programs with his ideas on personal and professional success.

He is one of only a handful of professionals to have earned the dual designations of *Certified Speaking Professional* (CSP) from the National Speakers Association and *Certified Management Consultant* (CMC) from the Institute of Management Consultants.

Frank graduated magna cum laude from Seattle University in 1972 with a degree in management while he was holding down a full-time job and he and his wife, Arnene, were raising six children. He has been a professional speaker and consultant since October 1974.

Frank is a lifetime honorary member of Rotary and is a member of Beta Gamma Sigma national business honorary as well as Alpha Sigma Nu national Jesuit honorary.

His work experience includes doing a hitch in the Navy, being a migrant worker, working in the mills, and being a carpenter's helper. Frank sold Fuller Brushes, served a six-year apprenticeship leading to his role as a journeyman printer, was part of the union leadership and part of newspaper production management, made monthly journeys into a maximum security prison, and served as Director of Religious Education for the Catholic Church. Today he is a professional speaker, an author, and a consultant to some of the world's largest corporations.

For information concerning Frank's speaking and consulting services, call or write to:

Frank Cooper
1411 Ballew Avenue
Everett, WA 98203
1-800-359-3719
1-206-353-2089
fjcooper@hotmail.com